# The Political Thought of
# Pierre-Joseph Proudhon

*To my father and mother*

Courtesy of Bibliothèque nationale

# The Political Thought
# of Pierre-Joseph
# PROUDHON

## BY ALAN RITTER

PRINCETON UNIVERSITY PRESS

PRINCETON, NEW JERSEY

1969

Publication of this book has been aided by the Whitney Darrow
Publication Reserve Fund of Princeton University Press

This book has been designed in Linotype Granjon

Printed in the United States of America
by Princeton University Press, Princeton, New Jersey

# Acknowledgments

Several institutions and individuals have helped me write this book. A Fulbright Fellowship in 1963-1964 enabled me to do research in Paris for the doctoral dissertation that was my first interpretation of Proudhon. Rethinking and rewriting were facilitated by grants from the American Philosophical Society and the Faculty Research Committee of the University of Virginia. The latter, along with the same University's Department of Government and Foreign Affairs, helped subsidize publication. Suzanne Berger read the first draft of the dissertation; Nicholas Wahl, Alexander Sedgwick and Dante Germino a late draft of the final manuscript. All four made helpful suggestions for improvements. I am also indebted to Pierre Haubtmann for valuable discussions on Proudhon and for access to unpublished material. My greatest thanks go to Stanley Hoffmann, whose advice and encouragement at all stages of my work were indispensable for its completion. None of these people can, of course, be held responsible for its content.

# Abbreviations

Listed below are the abbreviations employed in the footnotes for writings by Proudhon cited in the text. The dates within parentheses are the publication dates of the editions used. Whereever possible this is the new Rivière edition, eds. Célestin Bouglé and Henri Moysset (Paris, 1923 ff). Lacroix of Paris published those editions used which appeared prior to 1923. Where the original date of publication differs from that of the edition used here, the original date is given in square brackets. The English titles supplied below are my own, as are all translations from Proudhon's French sources, unless otherwise stated.

Dim.  *De la célébration du dimanche* (1926) [1839]. *On the Observance of the Sabbath.*

Prop.  *Qu'est-ce que la propriété?* (1926) [1840]. *What is Property?*

D.M.  *Qu'est-ce que la propriété? Deuxième mémoire* (1938) [1841]. *What is Property? Second Essay.*

Avert.  *Avertissement aux propriétaires* (1938) [1842]. *Notice to Property Owners.*

Ordre  *De la création de l'ordre dans l'humanité* (1927) [1843]. *On the Creation of Order Among Men.*

Carnets  *Les carnets*, 11 vols., written, 1843-1864. Volumes 1-5 and most of Volume 6 have been published, 2 vols. (1960). The others are scheduled for publication. The manuscript is in the Bibliothèque nationale. References are to the manuscript pages of both published and unpublished *Carnets*. The manuscript page numbers are given in the published text. *Notebooks.*

Cont.   *Système des contradictions économiques, ou philosophie de la misère*, 2 vols. (1923) [1846]. *System of Economic Contradictions, or Philosophy of Poverty.*

Mel.    *Mélanges*, 3 vols. (1868-1870), consists mainly of newspaper articles [1847-1850]. *Miscellaneous Works.*

Sol.    *Solution du problème sociale* (1868) [1848]. *Solution to the Social Problem.*

Conf.   *Les confessions d'un révolutionnaire* (1929) [1849]. *Confessions of a Revolutionary.*

Cours   "Cours d'économie politique," written, 1849-1855. References are to the page numbers established by Pierre Haubtmann and explained in his thesis, "La philosophie sociale de Pierre-Joseph Proudhon" (Faculté des lettres et des sciences humaines de Paris, 1961). "Treatise on Political Economy."

I.G.    *Idée générale de la révolution au dix-neuvième siècle* (1923) [1851]. *General Idea of the Revolution in the Nineteenth Century.*

R.S.    *La révolution sociale démontrée par le coup d'état du deux décembre* (1936) [1852]. *The Social Revolution Vindicated by the Coup d'Etat of December Second.*

Prog.   *Philosophie du progrès, programme* (1946) [1853]. *Philosophy of Progress.*

Justice *De la Justice dans la Révolution et dans l'Eglise*, 4 vols. (1930-1935) [1858]. *On Justice in the Revolution and in the Church.*

## ABBREVIATIONS

G.P.     *La guerre et la paix* (1927) [1861]. *War and Peace.*

P.F.     *Du principe fédératif* (1959) [1863]. *On the Principle of Federation.*

Cap.     *De la capacité politique des classes ouvrières* (1924) [1865]. *On the Political Capacity of the Working Classes.*

Corr.     *Correspondance*, 14 vols. (Paris, 1874-1875). *Correspondence.*

# Contents

CONTENTS

The Political Thought of
Pierre-Joseph Proudhon

Nous sommes bien plus appliqués à noter les contradictions, souvent imaginaires, et les autres fautes d'un auteur, qu'à profiter de ses vues, vraies ou fausses.—Vauvenargues, *Maxime* No. 622

# CHAPTER I

# Proudhon and His Interpreters

THIS book interprets Proudhon as a political theorist, through close analysis of his most systematic writings, and consequently differs in both method and aim from the standard studies of his thought. It differs in method by examining the consistency, truth, and meaning of Proudhon's ideas, without looking into their historical origins and effects. It differs in aim by arguing for the inherent merit of his theory, apart from its bearing on his personality or on the intellectual climate of his time.

The thesis of the book is that Proudhon, though a radical, was a realist and a moralist as well. His theory can therefore be regarded as an attempt to integrate these three divergent orientations toward politics into a tolerably coherent whole. The difficulties Proudhon encountered in this attempt are not his alone; they arise for any radical who faces facts and has a conscience. An analytic study of his writings should therefore clarify the problems of a sober and scrupulous kind of radicalism that will always be of interest.

The analytic approach to Proudhon adopted here is bound to arouse misgivings in those acquainted with the main interpretations of his thought, all of which, for different reasons, suggest that his ideas are too mistaken or confused to merit analytic treatment. Hence a helpful start for such a treatment is a review of the interpretations that seem to stand in its way.

Among economists, Proudhon has long been known as a self-taught dilettante, prolific in schemes for abolishing interest on money, but incompetent at economic science. Joseph Schumpeter well summarized this verdict: Proudhon realizes that his findings are "absurd," but, "instead of inferring from this that there is something wrong with his methods, [he] infers that there must be something wrong with the object of his research so that his mistakes are, with the utmost confidence, promulgated as results."[1]

Like the other interpretations to be examined, this one has more than a grain of truth. Many of Proudhon's explanations of social and economic facts are either untestable or else invalid by empirical scientific standards. But the weakness of his thought as social science does not disqualify it for analytic treatment. Proudhon does more than explain the facts; he makes conjectures and moral judgments about them. These non-empirical aspects of his thought show that standards other than those of science may be applied to it, which may well reveal that Proudhon's ideas are correct enough to merit analytic study despite their weaknesses from a scientific viewpoint.

Dismissal of Proudhon as an inept theorist is not widespread, except among economists. Most commentators

[1] Joseph Schumpeter, *History of Economic Analysis* (New York, 1954), p. 457. Vilfredo Pareto was of the same opinion, *Les systèmes socialistes* (2d ed., Paris, 1926), II, 275. One economic writer who disagreed with Schumpeter was Dudley Dillard. In his article, "Keynes and Proudhon," *Journal of Economic History*, II (May 1942), pp. 63-76, Dillard depicts Proudhon as Keynes' anticipator.

make no overt appraisal of his work and so cannot expressly call it worthless, but they disagree so much about its purpose that they too make critical analysis seem misplaced. When the most disparate goals have been plausibly ascribed to a theorist, it is natural to regard him as too muddled for analytic treatment.

The first goal ascribed to Proudhon was revolution. Those who did so saw him as a ferocious, atheistic, leveler, out to destroy bourgeois institutions, by violence if necessary, and to replace them with equal power and wealth for all. Proudhon's early pronouncements about property being theft occasioned this revolutionary image; his actions in 1848 confirmed it. Then, by siding with the proletariat against the bourgeoisie, and by extolling "the sublime ghastliness" of the insurrectionary "cannonade," he became known as *l'homme-terreur*. In a play of the period he figured as the snake, inciting Adam and Eve to revolt. A Daumier cartoon shows him, pickax in hand, demolishing the roofs of Paris. The caption reads: "The only way to destroy property."[2] Conservative writers have worked hard to perpetuate this image. As late as 1905 a book was written to expose Proudhon's subversive aim and to denounce his anti-clericalism.[3]

To Marxists, Proudhon's aim has seemed quite differ-

---

[2] For these and other details about Proudhon's rise to notoriety see Daniel Halévy's introduction to *Conf.*, pp. 36-43.

[3] Gaston Isambert, *Les idées socialistes en France de 1815 à 1848* (Paris, 1905), pp. 316-70. Other writers who have taken this view are: Martin Ferraz, *Histoire de la philosophie en France au dix-neuvième siècle* (3d ed., Paris, 1877), pp. 427-71; Arthur Desjardins, *Proudhon, sa vie, ses oeuvres, sa doctrine*, 2 vols. (Paris, 1896).

ent: to thwart a revolution, not to make one. The source of this contention is their master's dictum that Proudhon was a petty bourgeois. Marx never clarified his epithet, but this only made it more persuasive. Generally, the Marxists have claimed that whereas they want to press the class struggle to a definitive proletarian victory, "the petty bourgeois Proudhon opts for equilibrium, for mutual support of conflicting forces: the bourgeoisie is not to be abolished, but preserved by means of class collaboration."[4] To defend this reading they cite Proudhon's conciliatory attitude toward class conflict, his opposition to strikes, his qualified defense of private property (something the conservatives usually overlook), and his sympathy for *les petits*—those whose means of livelihood are independent but modest.[5] This view of Proudhon as a bourgeois counterrevolutionary seems more popular than any other and is accepted by many non-Marxists. Its popularity is no doubt due to the wide diffusion of Marxist ideas, which leave their mark even on those who reject them.

Still another goal has been ascribed to Proudhon by French reactionaries, who say his purpose was the same as theirs. This thesis was first suggested in 1909 by the anti-Semitic Edouard Drumont when he certified that "because of [Proudhon's] instinctive loathing of cosmopolites, he was the first of the nationalists."[6] A year later

[4] Henri Mougin, "Avant-propos" to Karl Marx, *Misère de la philosophie* (Paris, 1961), p. 15.

[5] See, e.g., Georges Cogniot, *Proudhon et la démagogie bonapartiste: un "socialiste" en coquetterie avec le pouvoir personnel* (Paris, 1958); E. H. Carr, *Studies in Revolution* (London, 1950), p. 44.

[6] Edouard Drumont, "Le centénaire de Proudhon," *La grande revue* (January 10, 1909), p. 140.

Charles Maurras confirmed this judgment: "Except in his ideas, Proudhon instinctively favored French [i.e. Maurrassien] policy."[7] Such pronouncements could hardly be convincing, since they deliberately ignored Proudhon's ideas. But this oversight did not last long. In 1912 the Cercle Proudhon, a leftish front for the Action française, began publishing its *Cahiers*, in which it tried to prove that its namesake was a forebear. The Cercle's most cogent spokesman was Georges Valois, then, as ever, eager to blur the line between left and right. "The core of Proudhon . . . is the artisanal, military and Christian thought of traditional, Catholic, classical France," he claimed.[8] At the center of this "core" Valois and his Cercle put Proudhon's patriarchic views on marriage and family life, his criticism of democracy, his peasant regionalism, and, above all, his French nationalism as typified by his stand with the pope against Italian unification. As for aspects of his thought that do not agree with this interpretation, "these outbursts are merely . . . an echo of contemporary ideas that he gave up bit by bit."[9] The Proudhon who emerges from this treatment may not be the most orthodox reactionary, but he seeks almost everything that they seek, except a restoration of the king.

The ideology most recently attributed to Proudhon has been fascism; the case for it rests partly on points made by the reactionaries and partly on points omitted by them.

[7] Charles Maurras, "A Besançon," *Cahiers du cercle Proudhon*, 1 (January-February 1912), p. 4.

[8] George Valois, "De quelques tentatives d'aggression contre le Cercle Proudhon," *Cahiers du Cercle Proudhon*, 2d series, 1 (January-February 1914), p. 80.

[9] *Ibid.*

Among the latter are Proudhon's occasional anti-Semitic remarks, his qualified support of Negro slavery, and his obscure attempt to persuade Louis Napoleon to reform society. When these aspects of his position are conjoined with those stressed by the Maurrassiens, Proudhon's ideas appear to be not just nationalistic and authoritarian, but racist and socialistic too. This version of his thought was first presented by the Nazis themselves, but it was most skillfully defended by an anti-fascist American; the French, however, have made only half-hearted attempts to support it.[10]

Proudhon's theory would not merit analytic treatment if two or more of these familiar portrayals of its aim could withstand critical examination, for then his theory would be proved a hopeless muddle. Fortunately, evidence abounds to refute all of these interpretations.

First of all, the biased concerns of the interpreters color their portrayals. Authors of theses about Proudhon's aim were not chiefly concerned with defining his thought fairly; what mattered most to all of them was the advantage they could win for their political positions by arguing for a particular concept of his objective. Conservatives, for instance, could hope to attract support from the political center by depicting Proudhon as a terrorist. Marxists, in contrast, might win converts among committed leftists by

[10] J. Salwyn Shapiro, "P.-J. Proudhon, Harbinger of Fascism," *American Historical Review*, L, No. 4 (July 1945), pp. 714-37. Karl Heinz Bremer, "Der sozialistische Kaiser," *Die Tat*, XXX (1938), pp. 160 ff; Willibald Schulze, "War Proudhon Anarchist?" *Deutschlands Erneuerung*, XXIII (January 1939), pp. 14-21; Jacques Bourgeat, *Proudhon, père du socialisme français* (Paris, 1943); Henri Bachelin, *P.-J. Proudhon, socialiste national* (Paris, 1941).

calling him an enemy of revolution. The reactionaries could use their identification with Proudhon both to attract leftists hostile to Marx and to distinguish themselves from those conservatives who thought that Proudhon was subversive. Fascists too could find advantages in equating Proudhon's objectives with their own, since this maneuver might win support among his sympathizers, whatever their place in the political spectrum.

These interpretations of Proudhon's thought, however, are not necessarily invalid; they might be accurate *despite* their authors' partisan concerns. But in comparison with what Proudhon himself said about his purposes, all of these interpretations miss the mark.

The conservatives' contention, that he was a revolutionary, ignores his well-known opposition to violence, as well as his explicit praise of the very inequality and religion that they see as targets of his attack.

The Marxist view of him as an enemy of the workers overlooks his many pronouncements in favor of the proletarian cause. This view also mistakes the reasons behind some of his positions, such as his opposition to strikes: Proudhon did not oppose strikes because he was devoted to class collaboration, but because he was suspicious of the trade union mentality which strikes so often induce among the workers.

The thesis of reactionaries that Proudhon was their forerunner does not withstand examination either. For one thing, this thesis totally neglects some of his most clearly stated teachings, such as his condemnation of tradition and the Church. The reactionary argument also twists the meaning of those of Proudhon's teachings it does consider. His opposition to Italian unification, for instance, was not a defense of Catholic objectives, as Valois implied, but of the small-scale governments that unification would destroy.

As for the view that Proudhon aimed for fascism, it too rests on a weak foundation. Fascists seek dictatorship, which Proudhon hated. Fascists spurn individual freedom, which to Proudhon was the greatest good. These differences between Proudhon and the fascists make the resemblances in their thought too superficial to serve as proof that their objectives are the same.

This is not the first time that the standard readings of Proudhon's aim have been deplored as caricatures. After the First World War the Société des amis de Proudhon was organized to develop and publicize a more accurate view of its mentor. To this group we owe thanks for the new critical edition of Proudhon's works, a great aid to the study of his writings.[11] The Société also published a useful collection of Proudhon's essays and several anthologies of his work. Probably most important was the group's encouragement of serious scholarship; some of the best recent studies of Proudhon have been written by authors connected with the Société.

But though the Société effectively challenged some interpretations, it did not altogether replace them with more acceptable ones, which is not surprising, since many of the group's adherents brought the same sort of partisan concerns to their studies of Proudhon that had animated previous interpreters of his thought. Some of the group,

[11] The edition would be even more useful if it had an index.

sympathetic with the French labor movement, equated Proudhon with the syndicalists, despite the fundamental differences between their ideas.[12] Others, like Armand Cuvillier, reworked the Marxist reading of Proudhon, while Daniel Halévy tried to make Proudhon an anticipator of his own highly personal outlook on politics.

It is true that not all associates of the Société brought partisan concerns to their writings on Proudhon; but these impartial portrayals of his theory are not much more satisfactory than the politically inspired ones. The scholarly Célestin Bouglé, for example, had no partisan motive for saying that Proudhon was a sociologist at heart; yet this interpretation, like that of the economists, ignores the normative and conjectural elements in his thinking. Other impartial writers interpret Proudhon inadequately for a different reason. Although they say nothing about the general character of Proudhon's theory and so cannot oversimplify it as Bouglé does, their unwillingness to characterize deprives them of a thesis to unify their vision of his work, and inclines them to focus so minutely on its details and background that they convey a fragmented and eclectic picture of it. Though these writers impose no artificial unity on Proudhon's theory, they find little unity in it of any kind.[13]

[12] For a thorough comparison of Proudhon and the syndicalists see Gaëtan Pirou, *Proudhonisme et syndicalisme révolutionnaire* (Paris, 1910).

[13] The work of such interpreters as Georges Guy-Grand and Edouard Dolléans, notwithstanding its unquestionable merit, does seem to suffer from this sort of eclecticism. See Georges Guy-Grand, *Pour connaître la pensée de Proudhon* (Paris, 1947) and Edouard Dolléans, *Proudhon* (Paris, 1948).

Since impartial commentators do find Proudhon inconsistent, while only biased and mistaken ones do not, it is tempting to conclude—which would be fatal to this study —that his theory is indeed confused. There can be no doubt that Proudhon is the kind of theorist who, because both his life and his writings are highly ambiguous, invites partisan and eclectic readings. But inconsistency does not preclude coherence. A look at the ambiguities that induce the inaccurate readings may reveal the possibility of an acceptable interpretation of his theory, despite its absence up to now.

Even Proudhon's early biography has supplied grist for the interpretational mill. Do you want to paint him as a peasant, rooted in the tradition of soil? Then you note that in his youth he spent long months alone in the fields tending cattle. Are you interested in depicting him as a petty bourgeois? Then you dwell on his father's marginal economic status as an impecunious and ultimately bankrupt brewer. If your aim is to portray a dangerous proletarian revolutionary, you can stress his early experience as a printer and his links with the insurrectionary secret societies of Lyons. And if you want to take a nonpartisan stand, you can acknowledge that all of these experiences influenced his thought and that all of them contribute to its inconsistency. Many other cases of ambiguous biographical influences could be mentioned, for they crop up throughout Proudhon's life. But enough has been said to show how these diversities are used to develop both the mistaken though coherent, and the accurate though unsynthesized, interpretations of the man and his thought.

Even a life as ambiguous as Proudhon's could not have

furnished enough material for his disparate images. The necessary supplement was provided by his writings themselves, for they are even less definable than his biography. As one commentator complained, "It is literally impossible to analyze not only his complete works but even his most important writings; . . . certain chapters are so turbid and diffuse that even the best informed reader is unable to discern any general point; and . . . the critic continually wonders if he is misrepresenting his author by citing a passage which is demolished with equal vigor ten pages later."[14] The apparent contradictions in Proudhon's work, more than anything else, explain why it invites polemical distortion and keeps conscientious critics from portraying it as unified. Proudhon's work seems inconsistent for several reasons, one being that it is resolutely unmethodical, since Proudhon was not, and did not wish to be, a systematic philosopher. "My aim is not to write a moral treatise, any more than a philosophy of history," he said in his most comprehensive work. "My task is more modest: first we must get our bearings, everything else will then follow automatically."[15]

Proudhon's incompetence in economics adds to the apparent inconsistency of his theory, by making an impor-

[14] Maurice Lair, "Proudhon, père de l'anarchie," *Annales des sciences politiques*, xxiv (1909), p. 589; cf. W. Pickles, "Marx and Proudhon," *Politica*, iii (1938-1939), p. 235: "Proudhon is . . . anything but a consistent thinker. . . . He presented the public with a running analysis of his own mental processes, he thought aloud in print, giving free reign to irony, invective, metaphor and every kind of passion as his feelings dictated. He corrected himself as he went along."

[15] *Justice*, i, 239; cf. *ibid.*, iii, 264; *Corr.*, xii, 317, 344.

tant part of it a muddle. In 1841, soon after publishing his second book on economics, he confessed to a friend, "Political economy is not my strong point and it will be most unfortunate if I have not given it up completely before I am forty."[16] His foreboding came true, because he dabbled confusedly in economics all his life.

Frequent polemical exaggeration is another of Proudhon's traits that make him seem inconsistent. It is common in the history of political theory for a writer to slant his position so as to sharpen its contrasts with that of his adversary. Proudhon often did this because he found polemical exaggeration difficult to avoid: "It is impossible for me to retain philosophical composure and indifference, especially when I have to deal with biased and dishonest opponents."[17] With most writers such a disposition does not lead to contradiction. Polemical exaggeration is usually aimed at only one, or at most a few, allied opponents; its excesses therefore produce parallel, not conflicting, distortions. But Proudhon found opponents everywhere. He thought himself "l'excommunié de l'époque."[18] "The development of my thought has deprived me of almost all community of ideas with my contemporaries," he explained.[19] Finding himself surrounded by enemies, all of whom opposed him for different reasons, he lashed out simultaneously in contradictory directions. In 1848, for example, being equally opposed to democrats, socialists, and conservatives, he assaulted all three with equal vigor. By doing so, he exposed himself to plausible charges by each adversary of sympathizing with the others. There

[16] *Corr.*, vi, 313.
[17] *Ibid.*, vii, 8.
[18] *Ibid.*, vii, 265.
[19] *Ibid.*, ii, 284.

are many other cases where Proudhon's attack on a variety of rival opponents made his own position seem self-contradictory.

Still further evidence of Proudhon's inconsistency is the fact that he altered his ideas over a period of time. His theory appears quite different depending on whether its early, middle, or late form is emphasized, while if all three phases are given equal weight, a composite and incongruous picture is likely to result. Though Proudhon usually denied that his position had evolved, its changes have often been pointed out by others. Indeed, a major purpose of Proudhon studies has been the charting of his theory in order to distinguish the fundamental from the circumstantial changes in his ideas. Scholars now agree that most of Proudhon's changes are circumstantial and that those occurring in the foundations of his theory involve shifts in emphases among fixed premises, not changes in the premises themselves.[20] But recognition of his fixed premises does no more than reduce the apparent inconsistencies in Proudhon's thought. Shifts of emphasis can produce almost as many incongruities as can changes in first principles. Even after basic continuities are acknowledged, the earlier Proudhon still cuts quite a different figure from the later Proudhon.

Because so much data suggests that Proudhon is incoherent, it is indeed hard to see the unity of his thought;

[20] Henri de Lubac, *The Un-Marxian Socialist* (London, 1948), p. 30, "Between his former works and those of the days of his exile, though there may be a few changes in tone or emphasis, we do not find the profound differences which some have thought they could see"; cf. the introduction to *P.F.* by J. L. Puech and T. Ruyssen, p. 75.

yet this data is weaker proof against unity than may appear. Consider first the biographical evidence offered for his inconsistency: Proudhon's varied experiences, however ambiguous, do not prove that his ideas are incoherent, since a man whose behavior is irregular can still think clearly. The same point applies to Proudhon's lack of system. An unsystematic writer may also be inconsistent, but he need not be. Inconsistency and lack of system do not always go together.

As for Proudhon's incompetence in economics, it neither confuses his political ideas nor thus precludes a unified political theory. In fact, as we shall see, even Proudhon's most muddled monetary scheme, rather than complicating his political problems, helps resolve them.

Nor are Proudhon's polemical exaggerations obstacles to coherent interpretation of his thought. It is usually quite simple to recognize these excesses and thus discount them as forensic tactics, so that they do not affect one's reading of his theory. This corrective technique no doubt deprives Proudhon's viewpoint of some of its panache, but this is a necessary and not excessive sacrifice to make for an accurate understanding of his position.

The doubts about Proudhon's consistency, based on his changing views, also can be allayed. As pointed out, these changes are only shifts in emphases among fixed premises, and although the changes reflect the development of his thought *around* a basic structure, they do not alter the structure itself, and so need not be considered in assessing the fundamental consistency of his thought.

Though the evidence examined thus far does not seem to rule out the feasibility of a unified interpretation of Proudhon, another kind of evidence might do so. Allegations against the consistency of the fundamental propositions in his theory must be examined. Proudhon's premises, arguments, and conclusions might be so thoroughly contradictory that any attempt to depict them as coherent would be futile. That there are conflicts among his basic propositions is certain; that there are logical inconsistencies is less clear. It may be that the conflicts among these propositions, rather than confusing his thought, give clues to its meaning. To find out, it is necessary to ask if his premises are logically opposed and if he contradicts himself when he applies them.

The value of asking these questions can be brought out by comparing the situation faced by the analyst of Proudhon's ideas with that confronting the student of Locke's. Their problems of interpretation are analogous, because both deal with theories containing similar contraries.

Locke's theory exhibits two conflicting trains of thought. On the one hand, his theory paints a harmonious picture of the state of nature and lays down generous terms for the right of revolution. Each citizen decides for himself when revolution is justified, by comparing his situation under government with the one he would enjoy in the state of nature. If the latter seems preferable to him, he is entitled to revolt. Interpreters who stress this side of Locke's theory usually view it as an attack on absolute government and a spirited defense of revolutionary overthrow. The Continental Europeans have traditionally depicted it in this way. C. E. Vaughan is a more recent espouser of this interpretation.[21]

[21] Vaughan very nearly makes Locke an anarchist, for in his view Locke "lays the State at the mercy of the individual, by enabling any minority, however small, to challenge the moral jus-

But Locke's theory has elements that suggest a different reading. Some parts of the *Second Treatise* stress the inconvenience of the state of nature instead of its harmony. Other passages make clear that the generous right of revolution is scarcely operational. Locke gives ample justification for revolt, but the institutions he prescribes make successful overthrow difficult to achieve. The interpreters who emphasize these elements of Locke's position come to quite a different conclusion about his theory: Locke appears to them as some kind of authoritarian, perhaps a majority rule democrat, perhaps a crypto-Hobbist.[22]

In reaction to both of these coherent but one-sided accounts, a third, eclectic approach may be pursued. The critic may describe both trends in Locke's thought, assign equal weight to each, and conclude that he is more or less hopelessly muddled.

But let us consider another interpretational option— also a reaction to the one-sided approaches—which begins by acknowledging that Locke's theory is rife with conflict but, unlike the eclectic view, does not conclude that it is contradictory. Instead, this fourth approach offers reasons for Locke's ambiguities and draws out their implications. By taking this approach the analyst is able to evince the dilemmas that plagued the founder of liberalism and that continue to perplex its adherents.

---

tification of any law." *Studies in the History of Political Theory before and after Rousseau* (New York, 1961), i, 168.

[22] These are the themes of two well-known studies of Locke. Willmoore Kendall, *John Locke and the Doctrine of Majority Rule* (Urbana, 1941); Richard H. Cox, *Locke on War and Peace* (New York, 1960).

It is obvious that the first three strategies used to construe Locke's theory correspond to the previously described strategies used to interpret Proudhon's theory. But the fourth approach, mentioned above, may apply to Proudhon as it applied to Locke. Explication and analysis of the conflicts in Proudhon's thought may evince the dilemmas which perplex a radical thinker and that confront his interpreters.

Pursuit of this approach requires that the character of Proudhon's conflicting premises be clearly understood. Comparison with Locke is almost as helpful for this purpose as for clarifying interpretational strategies, because Proudhon's most basic political conflicts are strikingly similar to Locke's. Locke's dilemma is to reconcile the constraints of social life with individual freedom. When he stresses the restrictions prerequisite for social living, his theory takes on an authoritarian tone; when he stresses the value of freedom, his theory sounds more libertarian. Proudhon's problem is precisely the same. He too values the reconciliation of liberty with social life and therefore frames a theory that sometimes stresses authority, sometimes liberation. But here the similarity between the two writers ends: Proudhon's ambivalence, though of the same kind as Locke's, differs vastly in degree. This all-important difference results from a more extreme conception of liberty, on the one hand, and a keener awareness of the need for social restraint, on the other.

Probably no one in the history of political theory has conceived of liberty more broadly than Proudhon, since none has required that men, to count as free, be unhindered by as many restraints. Certainly Locke's freedom, by comparison, is meager indeed. For him "liberty is to be free from restraint and violence from others . . . and is not, as we are told, a liberty for every man to do what he lists."[23] In Locke's view, men can be restrained in many ways without ceasing to qualify as free: they can be pressured socially, exploited economically, censored religiously, or repressed legally. Provided they are not "subject to the arbitrary will of another," they are free men in the full sense of that term. Locke even goes a step further. Certain kinds of restraint are included in the very definition of liberty. In the state of nature, man's liberty consists not just in his freedom from the will of others but also of his having "the law of nature for his rule," while under government part of the definition of liberty is having "a standing rule to live by."[24] A person who is unrestrained by such laws or rules is not freer than one who is. On the contrary, he is not free at all, for he is in a state of license, not liberty.[25] Freedom for Locke, then, requires only a limited absence of restraint and actually calls for the presence of certain impediments.

To Proudhon, on the other hand, "freedom" denotes total liberation, from every possible form of hindrance. The absence of other people's restraining wills is only a small part of liberty; the presence of any limitations, far from being a requisite for liberty, is an obstacle to it. A free man must be "liberated from all restraint, internal and external."[26] Both kinds of restraint are defined in very

[23] John Locke, *Two Treatises on Government*, ed. Peter Laslett (Cambridge, England, 1960), p. 324.
[24] *Ibid.*, pp. 301-302.      [25] *Ibid.*, pp. 288-89.
[26] *Justice*, III, 409.

broad terms. External restraint includes, in addition to the hindrances identified by Locke, every kind of legal, social, and natural impediment.[27] A man's freedom is restricted just as much by duly enacted laws, social pressures, religious codes, economic, and even physical forces, as by the arbitrary wills of other people. Internal restraint includes not just the tyranny of passion, but control by conscience. A free man "can resist even the voice of conscience and can do what he himself declares wrong and evil."[28] "He is able to dishonor his person, deprave his nature, and debase it further than could his passions, acting alone."[29]

This conception of freedom shows no trace of the traditional equation, implicit in Locke, of liberty and goodness. A man does not cease to count as free when he misbehaves, or even when he is unhindered by rules. In his famous hymn to liberty, "le génie de la révolte," Proudhon outlines the extreme implications of this position:

"Liberty recognizes no law, no motive, no principle, no cause, no limit, no end, except itself. . . . Placing itself above everything else, it waits for a chance to escape . . . all laws but its own, to insult everything but itself, to make the world serve its fancies and the natural order its whims. To the universe that surrounds it it says: no; to the laws of nature and logic that obsess it: no; to the senses that tempt it: no; to the love that seduces it: no; to the priest's voice, to the prince's order, to the crowd's cries: no, no, no. It is the eternal adversary that opposes any idea and any force that aims to dominate it; the indomitable

[27] *Ibid.*, III, 407.  [28] *Ibid.*, III, 418.  [29] *Ibid.*, III, 411.

insurgent that has faith in nothing but itself, respect and esteem for nothing but itself, that will not abide even the idea of God except insofar as it recognizes itself in God as its own antithesis."[30]

This passage is a key to Proudhon's thought. By committing himself to such a radical ideal of liberty, he placed a towering obstacle in the way of its realization. Any attempt to create a world where men can enjoy such unlimited freedom is bound to encounter grave problems. Examination of Proudhon's attempt to reach this objective therefore brings into sharp relief the theoretical difficulties of all extreme libertarian endeavors.

The other horn of both Locke's and Proudhon's basic dilemma is awareness of the restraints necessitated by social life. Here, as in his conception of liberty, Proudhon goes beyond Locke, thus further sharpening their shared ambivalence.

Locke recognized that, in the absence of all restraint, social life was inconvenient, but he believed it was both possible and preferable to extreme political coercion. He tried to reconcile social life and freedom by describing the state of nature as a feasible social arrangement that men could revert to as a refuge from intolerable oppression.

Proudhon could not adopt this solution because he thought it was chimerical. Locke's state of nature, like any social arrangement, is inescapably restrictive, for at least two reasons. First, human nature makes unrestrained social life impossible. "Man is naturally free and

[30] *Ibid.*, III, 424.

selfish, . . . capable of self-sacrifice for love or friendship, but rebellious."[31] Hence, if left unrestrained, people will not get on harmoniously: they will oppress one another. Second, and more subtle, the process of personal interaction necessarily imposes prevalent norms on each member of society. "I view society, the human group, as being *sui generis*, . . . with its own functions, foreign to our individuality, its ideas which it communicates to us, its judgments which resemble ours not at all, its will, in diametrical opposition to our instincts."[32] Since society influences its members directly, none can escape being restrained by the norms and expectations that prevail in it.

Both these points need further elaboration. Their interest here lies in the light they shed on the basic conflict in Proudhon's thought. Had he worked with an unexamined or even a Lockean conception of the need for social restraint in his effort to achieve total liberation, his difficulties would have been great enough. The problems raised by attempts at complete emancipation are themselves acute. But by identifying the unavoidable obstructions to such attempts, he increased his difficulties.

The conflict between these two basic premises—a radical concept of liberty and a realistic acknowledgment that restraint is unavoidable—made theorizing a Sisyphean labor for Proudhon: the closer he came to his goal of total liberation, the heavier his sense of the need for restraint weighed on him. Most of the incoherences in his thought, including many of those exploited by the polemicists and catalogued by the scholars, can be understood

[31] *Ibid.*, I, 306.     [32] *Prog.*, pp. 66-67.

as symptoms of this fundamental dilemma. By following Proudhon in his search for a resolution, I hope to present a unified account of his thinking that overlooks none of its ambivalence.

The work most useful for this purpose is *De la Justice dans la Révolution et dans l'Eglise*; it goes further than any other toward explicating and applying his first principles. This book, which is Proudhon's summa, will therefore be the main source for my interpretation. Other writings must also be considered, inasmuch as they clarify the views expressed in *Justice*. Of these, the most helpful is probably the "Cours d'économie politique," an unpublished work recently unearthed by Pierre Haubtmann. There, in curiously transfigured form, much of the theme of *Justice* can be found in embryo. Almost as important is the sequel to *Justice, La guerre et la paix*; though mainly devoted to international relations, it is more than obliquely relevant for domestic politics. These three works form a solid basis for a study of Proudhon that takes full account of his complexity.[33]

The plan of this book is suggested by its overall approach. The next chapter explores Proudhon's realistic awareness that restraint is unavoidable. The third chapter studies his radical contention that liberation of the individual ought to occur. The book moves on, in chapter four, to analyze the confrontation of restraint and liberation; when Proudhon's libertarian ideal faces his recognition of social realities, the result is an extreme critique of the existing world. Chapter five examines his attempt to

[33] Though *Propriété* is certainly his best-known book, it is not especially useful for this study, being quite unsystematic and unusually polemical.

combine the opposed tendencies of his thought by devising a socio-political arrangement for effectively reconciling freedom and social life. The last analytic chapter studies Proudhon's tactics: the means he used for reaching his chosen ends.

Though all these chapters are expository, they are not merely descriptive; they are more than a tidy reformulation of Proudhon's ideas. They comprise an effort at internal comprehension, designed to bring out the half-hidden implications of his thought. Following Raymond Aron's example, "we isolate his theory; in a sense, we complete his system."[34] This enterprise sometimes leads to asking questions that Proudhon did not expressly put, and to giving answers he did not explicitly provide. The risks of such a procedure are considerable; the reader must decide if it has compensating merits.

All of the chapters outlined thus far include evaluations of the points analyzed in them. The final chapter goes a step further by criticizing both Proudhon's way of posing the problem of liberation and his solution. There I sketch a different solution, suggested by the strengths and weaknesses of his approach. It is here that his theory may be of practical value, since an understanding of his position indicates some promising paths toward liberation and others to be avoided. But even if these practical suggestions are worthless, the theoretical value of studying Proudhon remains unimpaired. For however great his reputation as an activist, he is also a man of thought: he strives to elucidate questions that face us all.

[34] Raymond Aron, *La philosophie critique de l'histoire* (2d ed., Paris, 1950), p. 10.

— 25 —

## CHAPTER II

# The Realistic Basis of Proudhon's
# Political Theory

PROUDHON'S realism is inspired by dissatisfaction with his utopian predecessors. Like Marx, who admired and followed him here, Proudhon subscribes to the utopians' radical ideals but condemns their disregard of repugnant facts. The utopians wanted to reconstruct the world; in this they were perfectly right. Their error was "to perpetuate the religious dream by rushing off into a fantastic future instead of grasping the reality that crushes it."[1]

The lesson Proudhon draws from the mistake of his predecessors forms the basic precept of his realism: "It is not enough to criticize and deny the legitimacy of certain facts, it is also necessary to discover their cause."[2] An assessment of the limits placed on renovation by existing conditions is the first important task of social theory. To accomplish this task, Proudhon tries to uncover the individual and social forces that inevitably limit change. By defining and accepting these limits, he hopes to appraise without illusion the chances of improving the world.

But realism requires more than defining and accepting limits. Theorists who start out to explain the world all

[1] *Cont.*, I, 134; cf. *Avert.*, p. 220.
[2] *Ordre*, 318.

too often end by thinking it unchangeable. Proudhon attacks the laissez-faire economists for drawing precisely this conclusion; by mistakenly seeing "in each fait accompli an injunction against all possibility of change" they do nothing less than canonize the actual.[3] Hence a realist's second task is to prove the possibility of change, thus to preclude the inference that the existing order is, and must be, permanent. Proudhon tries to accomplish this task through study of the past. His hope is that scrutiny of historical forces will bear on his critical and reformative venture by revealing that potentialities for improvement are immanent in existing conditions.

### Human Nature and the Limits of Oppression

One way Proudhon attempts to protect his theory from utopian thinking is by identifying those fixed traits of character that unavoidably limit action and choice. He insists that "man has a constant, unchangeable nature"[4] and that its study can help avert fantastic proposals and unfounded criticisms. Marx sharply rebuked him for taking this position: "M. Proudhon is unaware that the whole of history is nothing but a continuous transformation of human nature."[5] What may have troubled Marx was the

[3] *Cont.*, I, 134; cf. *Avert.*, p. 192. Gunnar Myrdal has exposed the conservative tendencies of classical economics in *Value in Social Theory: A Selection of Essays on Methodology*, ed. Paul Streeten (London, 1958), pp. 158-59. "As long as economics keeps its valuations implicit and hidden, the utilization of [its] concepts will tend to insert into scientific work a do-nothing bias."

[4] *Prop.*, p. 167.

[5] Karl Marx, *Misère de la philosophie*, ed. Henri Mougin (Paris, 1961), p. 153.

suspicion that theories like Proudhon's, by assigning fixed traits to human nature, help support the oppressive status quo. Certainly there have been writers, such as Hobbes, who used the alleged facts of human nature to help justify permanent repression. It is also true that the phrase, you can't change human nature, is an old favorite of conservatives.[6] Whether Proudhon's psychology really makes him conservative can be decided only by finding out precisely which mental traits he thinks are fixed.

One attribute of human nature regarded by Proudhon as a cause of unavoidable social constraint is psychological egoism, the propensity of a man to aim for nothing but his own satisfaction. Even in his early writings Proudhon sometimes calls man incurably egoistic, but it is in *Justice* that he tries most seriously to support this claim.[7] Defenders of psychological egoism are hard put to explain instances of apparent altruism. People sometimes do things that not only cannot satisfy them but are even detrimental to their personal welfare.

In order to overcome this objection Proudhon deals with an example. Suppose, he says, a friend secretly entrusts me with a considerable sum and dies immediately thereafter. His family is rich, worthless, and only distantly related to him. Moreover, I have reason to believe that he planned to make me his legatee. Nonetheless, I return the money to his relatives. It is obviously difficult

[6] But writers who are not conservative use this phrase too, as the case of Erich Fromm shows. Cf. Myrdal, p. 10.

[7] For an early defense of psychological egoism see, *inter alia, Cont.,* I, 355.

to account for my behavior from the viewpoint of psychological egoism. Desires for self-satisfaction appear overwhelmingly on the side of keeping the money; only unselfish motives seem to favor returning it. Yet Proudhon argues that my motives for returning it are selfish. "I reflect . . . that established law in no way sanctions my greed, that an unexpected event could expose my secret, that then I would be dishonored, that it would be more than a little difficult to explain such a windfall."[8] It follows that if selfish desires are my motive for returning the money in this case, where unselfish motives seem so much more plausible, then these same selfish desires will also be decisive in more ordinary situations, where they are stronger, and unselfish motives are less pronounced.

This is all Proudhon says to show the truth of psychological egoism. It is not much of a proof; indeed, it is hardly an argument. It is only a repetition of the old view, systematized by Hobbes and made popular in France by la Rochefoucauld, that when I satisfy another person I always do so in order to satisfy myself in some way. This old view is difficult to defend. Of course we feel satisfied whenever we attain some goal, generous or selfish. But this fact does not mean that we act *in order* to obtain self-satisfaction. We all know of cases where we are not aware of acting from selfish motives. The advocate of psychological egoism would have to postulate unconscious motivation to make his theory fit such instances. This

[8] *Justice*, I, 420-21. For an extended commentary on this passage see Ernest Seillière, *L'impérialisme démocratique* (Paris, 1907), III, 288-90.

— 29 —

postulate cannot be proved; and since there is no good reason to accept it, psychological egoism must be accounted false.[9]

But to dismiss Proudhon's egoism as factually unwarranted would be to miss its point. His psychology is political, not empirical. It charts the limits of critical and reformative possibility, not the truth about the human mind. For this purpose, as Hume saw, factual accuracy is a disadvantage.[10] Political arrangements designed to operate with men of even moderately generous disposition will be vulnerable to threats from the few inordinately selfish men. It is therefore wise to criticize existing institutions, and propose new ones, on the counterfactual assumption that all men are egoists. This assumption helps Proudhon confine his criticism within realistic limits by ruling out denunciation of both selfishness and of some restraints upon it. It also helps him avoid extravagance in the reformative part of his theory by barring proposals that rely on benevolence to improve the world.

Proudhon sees egoistic hedonism as another fixed trait of human nature that necessitates restraint. Egoistic hedonism is the disposition to get more satisfaction from actions that benefit oneself than from those beneficial to others. Even if men were simple egoists, they would not be egoistic hedonists unless they found that actions directed toward their own benefit, rather than that of others, produced the greatest self-satisfaction.

[9] It has been refuted many times. For a thorough demolition see C. D. Broad, "Egoism as a Theory of Human Motives" in *Ethics and the History of Philosophy* (London, 1952), pp. 218-31.

[10] *Theory of Politics*, ed. F. M. Watkins (New York, 1951), pp. 157-58.

Proudhon's position on the truth of egoistic hedonism vacillated during the course of his career. In *Propriété* he thought egoistic hedonism inaccurate, if not completely false. Man is there called "the most sociable of animals," by which Proudhon means that he usually prefers to benefit others rather than himself, when he cannot do both.[11] In the *Contradictions* this doctrine of predominant generosity is replaced by a contrary doctrine that is no more plausible. Men not only prefer their own benefit to that of others; they favor disastrous kinds of self-satisfaction, such as immediate sensuous gratification and the pleasures of gratuitous malice.[12] As it does so often, *Justice* gives Proudhon's definitive view on this matter. There man is described as "both a pugnacious animal and a sociable one."[13] His desire to benefit others is relatively weak and "will not hold out for long against egoism's ferocity."[14] Men usually act to benefit themselves, not others, when they cannot do both. "The principle of self-interest alone rules the world, barely checked by fear of the gods and dread of punishment."[15]

Proudhon defends this slightly mitigated egoistic hedonism no better than he does simple egoism. Here too, he takes his stand dogmatically, revealing once more the limits of his psychological vision. But here again this defect, far from impeding his subsequent theorizing, actually supports it. The assumption that men are egoistic hedonists as well as egoists averts some utopian criticisms and proposals that could otherwise be made. Most nota-

[11] *Prop.*, p. 304; cf. p. 318.     [12] *Cont.*, I, 354, 358, 365.
[13] *Justice*, I, 416.     [14] *Ibid.*, III, 519.
[15] *Ibid.*, I, 308.

bly, the assumption rules out schemes of reform based on enlightened self-interest, for they assume the possibility of inducing people to benefit others in order to satisfy themselves.

The final trait used by Proudhon to explain the necessity of restraint is the weakness of conscience. He grants, and indeed insists, that man has a conscience, that he judges some actions morally good and others evil.[16] But he is far more concerned to show that such judgments do not greatly affect man's conduct. No doubt, in his early writings there are statements to the effect that virtue is knowledge, that people who know what is right automatically behave accordingly.[17] Traces of this view persist in his later works.[18] But the fact remains that as Proudhon's thought matured he became increasingly skeptical about the efficacy of conscience. *Justice* stresses what he had previously tended to overlook, that man is "able to resist . . . his conscience."[19] Moreover, such resistance is not a mere possibility; people frequently do in fact fail to practice what they preach. "This is the spectacle offered daily by improbity."[20]

Proudhon's explanation for the weakness of conscience rests on his other psychological assumptions. As an egoist, man's most powerful motive is the desire for self-satisfaction and personal profit. Yet conscience often urges a different course. When that happens, selfish motives almost always win. "The will, determined by consideration of the strongest interest, silences conscience."[21]

[16] *Ibid.*, III, 340.
[17] *Prop.*, pp. 320, 324, 339.
[18] E.g., *Justice*, II, 263.
[19] *Ibid.*, III, 418.
[20] *Ibid.*, III, 520.
[21] *Ibid.*, III, 520.

This thesis puts further restrictions on criticism and reform. By taking the frailty of conscience for granted, the thesis excludes the disapproval of people for not living up to their principles. More important, it rules out any scheme for improving matters that relies solely on moral argument. Since virtue is not its own reward, the reformative enterprise cannot be confined to the changing of ethical convictions, as it was for the utopians, but must also find a way to secure compliance with them.

Does Proudhon's analysis of human nature have the conservative effect, perhaps feared by Marx, of justifying submission to an oppressive status quo? Certainly it makes some constraint inescapable and to this extent is decidedly conservative. But the repressive implications of Proudhonian psychology are limited. It mentions only three traits that entail unavoidable restraints; a really conservative view of human nature would claim others. Moreover, even the three mentioned alter their manifestations. "Our malice," for instance, "changes form and style over time: the medieval lord plundered travellers on the highway and then offered them hospitality in his castle; the mercantile feudalist, less brutal, exploits the proletarian and builds poorhouses for him."[22] Though this statement offers no reason to suppose that limits on egoism can ever be abolished completely, it does imply that the existing controls on it need not be permanent. Thus Proudhon's psychology succeeds in sobering critical and reformative endeavor without requiring perpetual submission to established forms of restraint.

[22] *Cont.*, I, 362.

## Society's Invisible Restraints

Proudhon's sociology reinforces his view of human nature by uncovering social forces that place unescapable limits on thought and action. In his published writings, and even in his letters, sociological propositions are rare and incomplete. We are told repeatedly that "the stimulus of society" affects men's behavior and ideas, but learn little about the scope and limits of this stimulus, or why and how it occurs.[23] The hints of a theory of social psychology in Proudhon's published work whet our curiosity without satisfying it.

Fortunately, the "Cours" does much to clarify Proudhon's views. There we find that each social milieu affects character in a different way. "There are just as many clusters of ideals or interests, industrial or political units, workers' groups, teaching communities, etc., as there are real persons, i.e., wholes being completed, individuals being formed."[24] Moreover, since each man belongs to a variety of social milieux, he acquires a number of diverse character traits. "The honest Parisian is unrecognizable when dressed in his national guard uniform and surrounded by his comrades; and someone known for his gentle ways and his tolerant opinions, who becomes a judge or juror, will astonish you with his pitiless rigidity."[25] Here, in vivid outline, is a theory of social character. Proudhon sees that man is a role player who behaves and thinks differently each time he steps into a different milieu.

[23] See, *inter alia, Justice*, I, 323, 325, 420-21; *Prog.*, 67-68; *Corr.*, VII, 370.

[24] "Cours," 1-12 (4).        [25] *Ibid.*, 1-12 (3).

Proudhon also has an accurate explanation for role playing. Each member of a social group wins the approval of the others by conforming to the group's norms. Since it is "from the consideration of his fellows or from their contempt that the subject derives either contentment or discomfort," whenever a person enters a social milieu, he tries to make his conduct conform with its members' expectations.[26] The gentle father becomes a bellicose soldier in order to win self-satisfaction by enhancing his reputation among his military comrades and superiors.

But status seeking is not the only cause of role playing. Men usually go beyond conforming to the expectations of others in order to win approval, and do so because they think they should. Expectations do more than "penetrate the intellect," thus inducing calculated conformity; they also "penetrate the conscience for which they immediately become a superior authority, which, expressly or tacitly, with or without the legislator's declaration, are soon transformed into usages, [and] constitute morality and customs."[27] Here Proudhon grasps another important social fact. Men often behave as others expect because they accept such expectations and incorporate them into their own frame of mind. Soldiers may act ferociously not simply because they think praise from others is contingent on doing so, but also because they come to accept ferocity as a military virtue and would disapprove of themselves if they failed to display it. The practice of living up to expectations often leads to acceptance of the expectations as morally valid. Hence social control takes two equally important forms. Besides influencing behaviour and choice

[26] *Justice,* i, 295.        [27] "Cours," 1-14A (2).

externally, through rewards and punishments, it also affects them internally, by molding personal conviction into a replica of prevailing norms.[28]

By defining the limits placed by society on thought and action, Proudhon moved closer to excluding wishful modes of thought from his theory. He was thereby enabled to see that proposals to release men entirely from social restraints cannot be implemented and that wholesale criticism is just as futile as objection to the restraint imposed by the force of gravity.

But Proudhon does not move from acknowledging society's repressive force to affirming the unavoidability of submission to convention. He is careful to point out that the scope of society's unavoidable control is limited. It is true that people are compelled to become aware of their associates' expectations,[29] but this awareness is not compelling. They need not internalize social values, for "conscience grants men a right to judge that is prior to society's conventional existence."[30] Whether they accept others' norms or not, they need not follow them, since they are always free to disobey their consciences.

In sum, while social restraint is a universal and unavoidable fact, it is not an iron law. Resistance to any of its

[28] If David Riesman is to be believed, Proudhon understood social constraint even better than his shrewd contemporaries Mill and Tocqueville. According to Riesman, they saw social conformity resulting only from "fear of what people might say—conscious opportunism, that is," not from "the more automatic outcome of a character structure governed not only from the first, but throughout life, by signals from the outside," *The Lonely Crowd*, Anchor Book edition (New York, 1953), pp. 293-94.

[29] *Prog.*, p. 128.          [30] *Justice*, IV, 487; cf. I, 325.

impediments is always possible in principle, though, owing to men's desire for prestige, unlikely to occur in practice. Only efforts to escape society's influence entirely cannot succeed. Proudhon's sociology thus has the same effect on his critical and reformative endeavor as his psychology. It sharpens awareness of the intractability of social restraint without reaching the conservative conclusion that all of it is inevitable.

## A New View of History: From Savagery to Despair

History for Proudhon serves as an antidote to complacency and resignation by showing that oppression need no longer be accepted in its established form. In his hands the European past becomes the evolvement of repressive social and psychological forces to a point where they can be escaped.

The beginning of his story is the state of desires and moral beliefs in the absence of social influence. Under such conditions, he says, "the prevailing rule is the greatest good, what is called the *felicity maxim*."[31] In other words, men are ethical as well as psychological egoists; they not only do, but also think they ought to maximize their self-satisfaction, especially their enjoyment of prestige.

Why does Proudhon choose this asocial and egoistic condition as his starting point? Certainly not because he thinks history really begins this way. "It is only abstractly" that man "can be considered in a state of isolation and with no law but egoism."[32] Proudhon knows perfectly well that man's condition was social from the start, and

[31] *Ibid.*, I, 298.    [32] *Ibid.*, I, 323.

that he never was an ethical egoist. Perhaps his claims to the contrary are best interpreted as experimental hypotheses. Proudhon may assume that if he can show the possibility of liberation for men who start without social ties and with a selfish morality, he will also have proved liberation possible under more conducive initial conditions.

When men who feel entitled to everything that satisfies them try to reach their goals, they face a serious problem. Each expects the others to cater to his wants and defer to him but is unwilling to acquiesce to them. Therefore, whenever he tries to win service and consideration, "he collides with another man, his equal, who disputes with him for possession of the world and for the approbation of other men, who competes with him, who contradicts him, and, being an independent and sovereign power, opposes him with his veto."[33] Thus, at history's hypothetical starting point, everyone's attempts at goal attainment are unsuccessful.

Such a situation is reminiscent of Hobbes' state of nature: men with a narrowly self-regarding morality keep one another from reaching their objectives. But that Proudhon's point of departure is basically different from Hobbes' is shown by the way the dilemma is overcome. According to Hobbes, as Proudhon says, man is "drawn to a social and juridicial state by a simple calculation of interests." In Proudhon's view, however, man departs from the state of war not as a result of some rational esti-

[33] *G.P.*, p. 54.

mate, but because the experience of conflict and frustration leads to an alteration in his moral outlook.[34]

What happens, Proudhon says, is that as men vie with one another for prestige and subservience, their morality undergoes a gradual change. They come to think that those who are strongest and hence most successful in winning deference or submission ought to win it, and stop seeking it if they are unable to acquire any. Few parts of Proudhon's theory are more obscure than his explanation for this change. He tells us that primitive man "esteems nothing but bodily strength," presumably because it is only by using it that he can win the esteem and submission he wants and feels entitled to. But why should he approve of bodily strength when it is wielded by his rivals in order to oppress him? Proudhon does not say. Yet he insists that the egoistic morality prevalent at the start of history is soon replaced by what he calls the right of force, the view that "the extent of force determines that of merit, and consequently that of right."[35] What is still more surprising is his claim that this belief is accepted not only by the successful, but "penetrates even the slave's conscience."[36]

Proudhon's major concern, however, is not so much the cause of this change in ethical outlook as its consequences. Once people have accepted the right of force, social relations undergo a total change. The free-for-all battle characteristic of history's starting point is replaced

[34] *Ibid.*, p. 120. Proudhon's critique of Hobbes here follows Rousseau's.

[35] *Ibid.*, p. 89.        [36] *Justice*, III, 60.

by a harmonious hierarchy of wealth, power, and prestige at the top of which stand the strong. The hierarchy is stable and harmonious because all of its members have internalized the expectations of those at the top. Each lives up to his own principles and augments his own satisfaction by deferring and submitting to the strong in proportion to the disparity between his strength and theirs. The only kind of oppression that occurs in this primitive hierarchic community is imposed by the unquestioned force of custom, which is unperceived by the community's members. "Among primitive peoples . . . ideas were self-justifying; no one felt a need to certify them in any other way."[37]

But though spontaneous consensus at first makes society perfectly harmonious, it is too weak to prevent instability. So long as each member of society follows expectations, the structure will remain stable. But should anyone fail to conform, the whole system will be jeopardized. Deviant behavior is especially likely to occur at the hierarchy's two extremes. Those at the top, who arrived there owing to their superior strength, convert their personal privileges into an hereditary right. "The idea that force engenders force, that the strong are born strong, produces the institution of hereditary nobility."[38] Once such a caste has been established, the right of force is sure to be abused. Descendants of the original aristocrats will not all be the strongest members of their respective generations and so, according to the prevailing rule, should not enjoy special privileges. Even if they do happen to be the strongest, their protected social position will tempt them to exploit

[37] G.P., p. 126.     [38] Ibid., p. 185.

"the plebs much beyond what is permitted by the right of force," by demanding more submission and deference from the weak than is warranted by disparities of strength.[39] Those at the bottom of the hierarchy, disillusioned by the immorality of their betters, and cruelly oppressed by them, will no longer incorporate the right of force into their own frame of mind. "A slave is still a man. To refuse him all dignity, all morality . . . is to provoke his vengeance."[40]

Once the right of force loses the support of custom and tradition, social harmony is jeopardized. Growing conflict threatens society with a reversion to antagonistic free-for-all. But new forms of control arise, which are more effective than custom, that reinforce the crumbling social consensus and prevent this regression. These new controls are the religion and government of classical antiquity.

Under the sway of pagan religion, the right of force is reaffirmed at all social levels, as "force is glorified, consecrated, [and] deified in the form of human images,"[41] Paganism also strengthens the allegiance of the inferior to the established order. To begin with, it distracts the inferior from their grievances by absorbing them in religious devotions.[42] Next, it placates them by placing divinely sanctioned limits on the right of the strong to dominate them.[43] But since these limits prevent only the most outrageous abuses, religion must resign the inferior to their lot. "Why am I poor and oppressed, while others like me, who may even be worth less, command and enjoy themselves? It is fate that has so established things,

[39] *Ibid.*, p. 186.    [40] *Justice*, III, 33.    [41] *G.P.*, p. 89.
[42] *Justice*, I, 365.    [43] *Ibid.*, III, 33, 47, 60.

it assigns each of us our part.... Who would dare protest against its decrees?"[44] Yet even the preaching of resignation is insufficient. Religion's ultimate weapon is intimidation. By means of its "dogmas, its mysteries, its sacraments, its discipline, its terror, its promises," it frightens the socially inferior into staying in their place.[45]

The first effects of government, according to Proudhon, are similar to those of religion. It too is a "coercive force" that prevents conflict "between the weak and the strong."[46] But initially government contributes much less to stability than does religion. It is no more than a minor prop.

So powerful are the joint effects of religious and political authority that society's precarious consensus is revived. Men of all ranks again internalize the expectations of those at the top and accept the principle of the right of force. "Once that formula, such as it is, has been disentangled from naive primitive ideas, and has been embodied in a constitution, in a legal code and in articles of religious faith, . . . the mind embraces it with the full force of its conscience and its good faith."[47] What Proudhon thinks he is describing here is the virtue of republican Rome, whose citizen, he says, "believes in this kind of justice with all his soul."[48]

While the members of Roman society accepted the right of force, its hierarchy remained stable. But "as a result of political, economic and social change," consensus,

[44] *Ibid.*, II, 171.    [45] *Ibid.*, I, 366.

[46] "Résistance à la Révolution," reprinted in *I.G.*, p. 380; cf., *Justice*, II, 172.

[47] *Justice*, III, 529; cf., IV, 402.

[48] *Ibid.*, III, 558.

though propped up by religion and government, nonetheless disintegrated.[49] In the first place, inequality of wealth gradually increased. "The vast majority of the Empire's inhabitants were propertyless, tenants of the State, urban proletarians, slaves."[50] As they grew poorer, they became less inclined to accept beliefs that only contributed to their misery. They lived in "a state of revolt and hatred."[51] Consensus disintegrated horizontally, on territorial lines, as well as vertically, on those of class. As the Empire expanded, the incorporated alien peoples grew less and less willing to accept Roman dominance.[52] Finally, even those at the top of the hierarchy and at the center of the Empire, for reasons not specified, ceased believing in their own principles. Perhaps awareness that their values were no longer accepted by their inferiors encouraged doubt of their validity.

Pagan religion proved unable to prevent this disintegration, because it put inadequate limits on the rights of the strong. While inequality was moderate and the Empire's boundaries narrow, paganism contributed to their acceptance. But when these increased, it could no longer check "the odious exaggeration of personality." Hence during the Empire's decline, paganism justified the elite's thirst for oppressive privileges and so helped erode consensus.[53]

When pagan religion could no longer manage social conflict, government had to do the job alone. But without the aid of religion, political regulation was very difficult. In the past, pagan myths had won unanimous acceptance for the law of the land, so that government had only

[49] *Ibid.*, III, 529.    [50] *Ibid.*, II, 11.    [51] *Ibid.*, III, 461.
[52] *Ibid.*, III, 561-63.    [53] *Ibid.*, I, 370.

to administer supplementary external sanctions for rules. Now people cared nothing for the law. "Man comes to consider laws and institutions as fetters imposed by force and necessity, but without roots in his conscience."[54] No longer able to rely on internalized acceptance of the law, "the government, compelled to use more and more force, turns toward despotism." Such a move is self-defeating. "Because of its violence, it loses the support society once gave it," and so must inflict continually harsher penalties.[55]

At this point men are indifferent or hostile to established institutions. They no longer share compatible expectations, desires, or values. One might suppose that people in such a frame of mind would obstruct one another's action so much that the established hierarchy would collapse. But for reasons not fully explained, this does not happen. The result of men's feelings of indifference and hostility is not revolt and conflict, but isolation and resignation. Persons of all ranks are overcome by what Proudhon calls a despairing consciousness, exemplified by Stoicism and Epicureanism, which prompts them to withdraw from contact with others and submit to laws of which they disapprove. "Each understands that he needs the others and that society cannot subsist without rules."[56] Hence all remain law-abiding and cooperative enough to prevent social chaos.

But though the despairing consciousness wards off immediate collapse, it also makes ultimate collapse more probable, by encouraging selfishness and accelerating the trend toward inequality. "Behind a peaceful exterior, so-

[54] *Ibid.*, III, 530.     [55] *Ibid.*, II, 177.     [56] *Ibid.*, III, 532.

ciety is in a state of war; it is being consumed by its own flames."[57] It is only because Christianity replaces paganism as the dominant religion that Roman society does not disintegrate.

Christianity, to Proudhon, is an improvement on paganism because it is better able to keep the privileged from abusing their rights. This it accomplishes with the dogma of original sin, which proclaims that "man, as the author of evil, cannot by himself have any rights."[58] Since no one is entitled to rights, those in high positions have none to abuse. But by the same token, those in low positions would seem to have no justification for submitting to their betters. The Church gets around this difficulty with the dogma of grace, according to which a Christian must endure "mortification and discipline. . . . It is only at this price that he can hope for . . . remission of his sins and answers to his prayers."[59] Though no one is entitled to rights, anyone possessing some is presumed to have received them by divine decree. "The inferior respects in the superior not a man but an officer of God."[60]

Under Christianity's stabilizing influence, men reacquire compatible values and resume following prevalent expectations. The main difference between dominant social attitudes at this period and in antiquity is that piety is more highly esteemed. "The value of a man is no longer

[57] *Ibid.*, III, 533.     [58] *Ibid.*, I, 394.     [59] *Ibid.*, I, 396.
[60] *Ibid.*, I, 405. Proudhon interprets other relevant Christian tenets in the same way. The doctrine of providence is a milder and hence more effective version of paganism's fate, *ibid.*, II, 193. The Church's teachings about the charitable duties of lords to serfs are a watered down and thus more acceptable version of pagan pronouncements about masters' duties toward slaves, *ibid.*, III, 60.

measured by his social and positive qualities, but by the rigor of his penance and the intensity of his expiation."[61] Inferiors therefore serve and defer to their betters because the latter are pious, and because they show their own devoutness by doing so. The major difference in politics between Christian and pagan times is a similar growth in religious influence. Formerly magistrates were superior to priests in power and prestige, now "it is the priest who has precedence over the magistrate."[62] The conversion of secular government into theocracy is accompanied by a change in social institutions. Monasteries and charities are founded, encouraging acts of devotion and altruism.[63] These changes are only matters of degree. Proudhon stresses the similarities far more than the differences in the institutions of the pagan and Christian eras. In both periods, they mold desires, values, and expectations in a way that stabilizes an inegalitarian society.

For Proudhon, Christianity's fall, like its rise, resembles paganism's. He sees Christian society as suffering from the same upsurge of inequality that had plagued the ancient world. Charities enriched priests; monasteries bred monkish parasites; the feudal system evolved so as to grant the nobility more and more power, wealth, and prestige.[64] Theocracy, which like the Roman Republic was established "in good faith to serve as a protector of rights," was led like the Empire "to set rights aside" in order to maintain the growing hierarchy.[65] Behind the

[61] *Ibid.*, I, 399.      [62] *Ibid.*, I, 396.
[63] *Ibid.*, II, 16, 18; III, 55, 59.    [64] *Ibid.*, II, 25, 54, 196, 222.
[65] *Ibid.*, II, 179.

trappings of divine right, the modern state grew increasingly despotic and arbitrary.

These trends had the same consequence as they had in antiquity. The first glimmerings of the Enlightenment mark the start of a period of despair, as men begin criticizing principles and practices that seem to justify and exacerbate oppression.[66] But Christianity is a stronger social cement than paganism; its dogmas are more firmly internalized. It therefore maintains hierarchy far more successfully than its predecessor. Even the French revolutionaries, who like the Church fathers aimed to overthrow the status quo, were content with surface changes in the political setup and unlike their forebears, failed to challenge the system's religious keystone. At the outset the Revolution did attack the Church, but at its height, under Robespierre, it declined again into hierarchy and religion.[67] The revolutions of 1830 and 1848 were just as unsuccessful; they were even more purely political and actually worsened conditions by aggravating governmental instability.

[66] In earlier versions of Proudhon's history, the Enlightenment, and its predecessor in his eyes, the Reformation, receive a different and more elaborate treatment than in later accounts. They are then portrayed as important anticipations of the French Revolution. See "Toast à la Révolution," reprinted in *Conf.*, p. 400, also *Mel.*, II, 22.

[67] *Conf.*, pp. 62, 88, 113; *I.G.*, pp. 125-27, 178, 220-36; *R.S.*, pp. 129-32; *Justice*, II, 36. Proudhon admits that many immediate causes help explain why the Revolution propped up religious institutions. He mentions the military threat, the menace of the Enragés, and food shortages; *I.G.*, p. 229; *R.S.*, p. 131; *Mel.*, II, 29. But he also insists that the Revolution would easily have overcome these difficulties without resort to religion, if men had unequivocally given up their old ideals.

Because the Revolution aborted, the despairing consciousness grew stronger. According to Proudhon, in his day as in late Roman times, men of all ranks, while no longer accepting conventional morality, nevertheless continued outwardly to conform so far as necessary to prevent chaos and permit pursuit of private, self-regarding activities. He composed a number of jeremiads describing the contemporary version of despair. In these strange outpourings, which mix lament with denunciation, the most typical manifestations of despairing consciousness, analogous, Proudhon implies, to Stoicism and Epicureanism in antiquity, turn out to be romantic aestheticism and the obsessive quest for wealth pursued by those who follow the accepted meaning of Guizot's "enrichissez-vous."[68]

Proudhon's bracketing of the mutually hostile aesthetes and philistines is certainly paradoxical, but from his perspective it is logical, since both groups share the attitude of withdrawal from the world he is anxious to emphasize. Romanticism, "which naturally expresses the desolation of a soul caught between an unrestorable past and an impenetrable future," is clearly withdrawn when it espouses art for art's sake, for then it expressly denies the importance of public life.[69] Romanticism is no less so, Proudhon maintains, when it takes a more activist line. The romantic prophet or reformer does indeed concern himself with his social milieu, but not as with something worth political attention. Instead, he treats it as an aesthetic object to be beautified for his own gratification, or at most, for that of his coterie.[70] As for the philistines, they, with

---

[68] *Conf.*, 360; *Justice*, I, 250-55; III, 535; *Corr.*, VII, 96.
[69] *Justice*, IV, 452.          [70] *Ibid.*, III, 641-42.

their cash nexus mentality, are even less concerned with social conditions. Though they withdraw to seek profit instead of beauty, their attitude, like that of the romantics, amounts to refusal to face the world's real problems.[71]

### History and the Prospects for Liberation

Although Proudhon's study of history is supposed to prove that liberation of the individual has at last become a possibility, his narrative seems to offer extremely meager hope for such a prospect. It is a story of perpetual constraint, having only cyclical variations, which ends, as it begins, with the imminent threat of even greater oppression. As Proudhon himself admitted, mankind has experienced nothing but "reactions and declines; it passes more or less lengthy periods in a continual going and coming."[72] Between what might be considered the two high points of Proudhonian history—Republican Rome and the early Christian era—there is really nothing to choose. "Here as then it is still the principle of authority that dominates."[73] If man is as oppressed today as at the dawn of history, what reason is there to think that the current period of despair will result in anything better than another epoch of internalized repression? One of Proudhon's answers to this question is based on an examination of history's pattern. He tries to show that the same occurrences which men found oppressive in their own lifetimes had unintended eventual consequences of which they were unaware but which form a trend favorable to liberation.

[71] *Ibid.*, III, 14-46.   [72] *Ibid.*, III, 512.
[73] *Ibid.*, II, 222; cf. I, 410.

If we compare the desires, values, and expectations of primal man with those of our contemporaries, Proudhon notes, we cannot help seeing that they have changed appreciably. The first men were scarcely aware of their behavior's consequences and acted without deliberation, like sleepwalkers.[74] Primal man was lazy, unwilling to work if he could avoid it. Most important, he was the sort of egoist who both desired and felt entitled to satisfy all his wants, especially his craving for the esteem of others. Proudhon's contemporaries, like ours for that matter, do not, as a rule, have these traits. They act deliberately, are not especially lazy, and do not feel entitled to universal deference and subservience. They have become foresighted and industrious, have acquired at least a rudimentary sense of fair play and impartiality, and have moderated their demands for esteem and submission. These changes in character indicate that men are now more apt for coercionless social life than before, and show that the chance for liberation has increased.

This conclusion is borne out by the pattern of development undergone by the major institutions: hierarchy, government, and religion. In the beginning all three helped bring about changes in man's character. Inequality of wealth extirpated laziness: "If the property owner had tired of appropriating, the proletarian would soon have tired of producing, and savagery, hideous poverty, would have been at the door."[75] Government produced changes in morality "by means of its tribunals and its armies," which "gave to the sense of right, so weak among

[74] *Ibid.*, III, 72.
[75] *Cont.*, II, 403; cf. *R.S.*, p. 137; *Carnets*, X, 357.

the first men, the only sanction intelligible to fierce characters."[76] Religion, especially Christianity, helped most in this transformation, just as it was the major source of oppression. If man was to shed his selfishness, "his intractable personality had to be tamed by the discipline of terror; and since that discipline could be produced only in religious form, it was necessary to replace a religion of pride [paganism], with a religion of humility."[77]

This process of character alteration is not easily reversed. Hence the closer repressive institutions came to achieving it, the more superfluous, and even detrimental, they became. A time ultimately arrived, put by Proudhon somewhere in the immediate past, when their contribution to this process was complete.[78] At that point, they still stabilized society, but no longer in any sense improved it.[79] The status of established institutions at this stage is succinctly described in an unpublished note about government: "Government was progressive when it defended a society against savages. There are no more savages: there are only workers whom the government continues to treat like savages."[80]

The pattern of institutional development thus points to the same conclusion as that of character development. In the course of history, repressive institutions gradually completed their task of "educating conscience and reason."[81] Having completed it, their discipline has become less beneficial, while the danger of escaping it has also

---

[76] *I.G.*, p. 374.    [77] *Justice*, I, 396.    [78] *I.G.*, p. 365.
[79] *Ibid.*, p. 226; *Justice*, II, 267.    [80] *Carnets*, VII, 219.
[81] *G.P.*, p. 345.

been reduced. Liberation has thus finally become a realistic goal.

Proudhon has another kind of argument for the possibility of liberation, besides those based on consideration of history's pattern. This is an argument about the basic cause of historical oppression. It begins by distinguishing the episodes in the historical process during which oppression was intensified. This happened, Proudhon thinks, whenever men became critical of established institutions but, due to despair, at first left them alone and then made changes that only stabilized them. Such events figure repeatedly in his narrative—in his portrayal of the late Roman period, the Enlightenment, and his own time.

It is his contention that the same explanation accounts for all three of these episodes, and hence for oppression itself. What happens each time is that the disparity between ideal and reality causes men to lose their commitment to both. They see the increasing divergence between existing institutions and the principles that inspire them. The sense of scandal produced by awareness of this gap leads to rejection of the actual as unfaithful to the ideal and repudiation of the ideal as inapplicable to reality.[82] Men lose their enthusiasm for the status quo without acquiring any compensating reformist zeal. Lacking resolve either to change or accept the world, they lapse into a state of despair whose outcome can only be intensified oppression.

By exposing the cause of historical oppression Proudhon

---

[82] *Justice*, iii, 537-38, 546. In Robert Merton's suggestive classification they are "retreatists," *Social Theory and Social Structure* (Glencoe, 1957), pp. 153-55.

thinks he has laid a basis for escaping it. "Now that we know what makes society move . . . , it is permissible to foresee that liberty, duly averted, will no longer be entranced by the idols of egoism."[83] We can finally become the masters of history, provided we no longer lapse into despair when faced with a gap between the ideal and the actual. If instead we perfect our ideals in the light of reality and improve the actual so that it conforms to our revised ideals, we will at last be able to move down the road toward liberation.

To this argument there is an obvious rejoinder. All that it seems to see as needed to escape oppression is an understanding of its historical cause. Such a view is unconvincing, since there are surely other, more formidable bars to liberation than simple ignorance. This objection can be overcome with an inference from Proudhon's other argument for the contemporary feasibility of liberation, based on consideration of history's pattern. It is reasonable to infer from this argument that unless history had advanced sufficiently, understanding of the historical cause of oppression would be unavailing. For in that case, neither character nor institutions would have evolved enough to make liberation either safe or desirable. Viewed in this light, Proudhon's two arguments for the possibility of liberation reinforce one another. The argument drawn from the pattern of history puts a late *terminus a quo* on the period when the one based on the cause of oppression is applicable, and strengthens its force within that period. This is precisely what Proudhon wants to do, since his aim is to show that liberation is possible now, not

[83] *Justice*, III, 540.

that it could have occurred at any time, if only someone
had been clever enough to discover the historical cause
of oppression.

## The Validity of Proudhonian History

No more than other histories can Proudhon's be judged
solely by its truth. Even if all the statements in his narrative were true, it still might not be valid. For the true
statements it contained might fail to shed light upon the
past.[84] Hence Proudhon's history must be judged by two
different tests. Its particular statements must prove true,
and its combination of statements must prove plausible
and suggestive. When tested in these ways, his reading of
the past has at least as many strengths as weaknesses, especially when compared with contemporary alternatives.

Perhaps none of its factual contentions is more doubtful
than its claim that uncivilized man was lazy. Proudhon
seems to have said this because he believed that indolence
prevailed among extant primitive peoples.[85] But this is not
true, and there is no reason to think the first men were
lazy. We should perhaps not be too harsh with Proudhon
for his belief in primal indolence. This thesis has been
axiomatic in Western social thought, at least since the late
eighteenth century. From Malthus to Freud a long series
of writers have assumed that primal man was lazy.[86]

[84] For defense of the point that truth is not the only test of value
in history, see William Dray, *Philosophy of History* (Englewood
Cliffs, N.J., 1964), pp. 27-35, and W. H. Walsh, *Introduction to
Philosophy of History* (London, 1951), Ch. 5.

[85] *Cont.*, I, 161.

[86] Riesman, p. 300.

Though there may be other patently false statements in Proudhon's history, there are even more dubious ones, for instance, his claim that the Enlightenment was an epoch of despair, during which people lost their allegiance to both ideals and reality. Though there is surely some evidence for this contention, much also counts against it. Questions about the validity of Proudhon's account are clearly raised by its affirmation of this and other statements of doubtful truth.

Inclusion of such dubious assertions does not in itself disqualify his account. Factual uncertainty is a characteristic of many statements about the past, especially general ones. Provided that Proudhon had considered the historical evidence adverse to his contentions, if only to refute it, his title to include them would have been clear. Unfortunately, he does not always do so. Sometimes he engages in special pleading by stressing the facts that confirm his remarks while ignoring unfavorable ones.

One of these dubious assertions calls for special consideration, because of its importance for his account and the questionable way it is supported. This is his statement that hierarchy and government once performed advantageous functions but no longer afford any benefits other than the maintenance of order. Evidence against this dictum is not hard to find. No matter how much harm they do, government and hierarchy still contribute *something* positive to well-being.

Proudhon's answer to this objection is unsatisfactory.[87] What he says is that although hierarchy and government

[87] See for instance, "Résistance à la Révolution," reprinted in *I.G.*, pp. 376-80.

may indeed have positive advantages, a time has come when these advantages can be produced by non-political means. The trouble with this argument is that it is circular. Its purpose is to confirm the proposition that liberation from government and hierarchy has become possible by showing that these oppressive institutions no longer make positive contributions. Yet it purports to prove that they no longer contribute positively by showing that liberation from them has become possible. The argument uses its own conclusion as a basic premise and thus reduces itself to a mere tissue of assumptions.

Perhaps most of the statements in Proudhon's history emerge from this examination sufficiently unscathed to be deemed not false. Can his historical perspective as a whole also withstand criticism? The test here, it will be remembered, is not truth, but plausibility and suggestiveness.

One recurring denial of the suggestiveness of Proudhon's account points to its neglect of economic development as a historical force, and a force which, as Marx showed, has liberating effects. Proudhon seems to pay close attention to economics in *La Guerre et la paix*. He even asserts that poverty is *the* cause of both war and revolution.[88] His position has led some commentators to claim him as an economic determinist.[89] Unfortunately, this interpretation overlooks his continual insistence that poverty, far from being a causal ultimate, is itself determined by non-economic forces. "It is neither capital nor com-

[88] *G.P.*, pp. 358-60; cf. *Cont.*, II, 102.
[89] See for instance, Henri Moysset's introduction to *G.P.*, p. xxvii.

merce that governs the world, despite what we hear."[90] Poverty "is an essentially psychological fact: its source lies, on the one hand, in the idealism of our desires, and on the other, in our exaggerated sense of our own dignity and our slighting that of others."[91] Here Proudhon traces the cause of his alleged economic determinant back to the same forces that animate his narrative. By doing so, he betrays a historical vision that does ignore the role of economic development. To the extent that this neglect impoverishes his interpretation of history, it counts against its validity.

Whatever the defects of this oversight, Proudhon's outlook has some compensating merits, especially when compared with nineteenth-century alternatives. Most of its strengths stem from the limited purpose it was meant to serve. Proudhon, unlike many of his contemporaries, did not wish to write a speculative philosophy of history, designed to uncover the pattern, goal, and "meaning" of the entire past. His mistrust of philosophical history helped him avoid some common implausibilities, as is made clear by the difference between his view of history and that of its leading philosopher, Hegel.

Hegel's wish to understand the past as a whole leads him to claim that the pattern of historical change can be known a priori, rather than by induction from the facts.[92] Proudhon, on the other hand, has a more modest view of the method for understanding the past. The a priori "in

[90] *Carnets*, v, 122.
[91] *G.P.*, 347.
[92] G.W.F. Hegel, *Reason in History*, trans. Robert S. Hartman (New York, 1953), p. 79.

no case can become the direct object of our study." Historical writing must "consist exclusively of descriptions of phenomena and formulations of laws."[93] To say that the past reflects an a priori pattern is to exaggerate man's inability to control events and to make the prospects for liberation seem dimmer than they are in fact.

Hegel's belief in history's a priori pattern was by no means accepted by all philosophers, but his related opinion that the course of events has a praiseworthy end was more widely shared. In his early years Proudhon agreed that history has a morally desirable outcome. He even criticized Condorcet for denying that events would ever reach the praiseworthy goal he admitted they were tending toward.[94] But Proudhon's early position was both implausible and in conflict with his libertarian ideal. For if history is a road down which men must travel, then they cannot be free to diverge from it. It is therefore not surprising that by the time he wrote *Justice* he had reversed his opinion on history's destination: "We are not advancing toward an ideal of perfection, toward a definitive condition. . . . Since humanity is being endlessly renewed and developed, . . . the ideal of Justice and beauty that we must realize is always changing."[95]

Hegel not only claimed that history had a praiseworthy and attainable goal, but also that the route to it, and the pace at which it was traveled, were set by laws. In his

[93] *Justice*, III, 171.

[94] Pierre Haubtmann, "Pierre-Joseph Proudhon: sa vie et sa pensée" (unpublished thesis for the Doctorat d'Etat, Faculté des lettres et des sciences humaines de Paris, 1961), p. 282, annex 17.

[95] *Justice*, I, 233.

view one cannot skip over a particular stage of evolution "any more than one can skip over the earth." The "inner development of the idea" obeys fixed, unalterable rules.[96] If men try to break them, the cunning of reason sees that events nonetheless take their prescribed course. Since Proudhon's main objection to Hegel's a priori teleology was that it leaves no place for human freedom, it is not surprising that he was especially hostile to Hegel's explicitly deterministic doctrines. No doubt, at the outset of his career, he tended to agree with Hegel. In the *Contradictions* he announced that "humanity, in its development, obeys an inflexible necessity."[97] But this strict determinism is missing from Proudhon's mature thought. *Justice* still admits that unalterable laws partially control the course of events, but insists that voluntary action has even more influence.[98]

Hegel's determinism is especially distasteful to Proudhon, because it is concealed behind a pretense of freedom. According to Hegel universal history is the story of growing liberty. But the Hegelian conception of the process of change really leaves no room at all for freedom.

[96] Hegel, pp. 37-39.

[97] *Cont.*, I, 385. Proudhon qualifies this statement by saying that men can act as they choose and that their choices influence the course of events, *ibid.*, I, 387. But he immediately takes back the libertarianism implicit in these qualifications. The same sorts of events occur whether or not men want them to, though their timing and form may differ. Moreover, any aberrations imposed on historical development by men's voluntary actions can be foreseen in advance. (Proudhon does not say by whom), *ibid.*, I, 388.

[98] *Justice*, III, 151. It must be admitted, however, that notes of inevitabilism crop up in writings subsequent to *Justice*, e.g. *G.P.*, p. 202.

In spite of his libertarian pose, "everything for this German is organic evolution. . . . Development is always regulated by an inflexible reason" which "operates unknown to us, despite us, and, if need be, against us."[99] Since any genuine movement toward liberation "consists not of mankind's inevitable evolution, but of an unlimited emancipation from all inevitability," Hegel's views on freedom are a fraud.[100]

Although Proudhon's outlook on the past is impervious to Hegel's general, speculative ideas about how and why events take place, it does have affinities with his more specific and empirical views on these matters, and in this area of overlap are found the most suggestive parts of Proudhon's historical vision.

Both writers stress the interaction of personal and publicly established standards in their models of change. The motor of history for both of them is the successive conflict and conciliation of subjective values and external norms.[101] This focus of attention is extremely fertile, for it reconciles two seemingly incompatible ways of looking at the past. From this standpoint, history makes equal sense as a story of personal intentions and as the development of cultural

[99] *Ibid.*, III, 501.

[100] *Ibid.*, IV, 431. It seems likely that Hegel's philosophy of history is less deterministic than Proudhon suggests. See the forceful arguments to this effect in Dray, Ch. 6. Yet even if this is the case, Proudhon's objections to Hegel are not misplaced. His own position still remains less deterministic than Hegel's.

[101] For an analysis of Hegel stressing the importance of this interaction, see John Plamenatz, *Man and Society* (London, 1963), II, 200.

trends, because each of these phenomena is viewed as dependent on the other.

Proudhon's history, like Hegel's, also emphasizes the importance of recognition. For both, men's desire for the good opinion of their neighbors is a crucial datum of history; for both, this desire has a similar outcome. As people vie for prestige they come into conflict. This experience of conflict leads slowly to a growth in empathy and impartiality as men come to realize that they can win esteem for themselves only if they are willing to grant esteem to others. The desire for prestige is thus shrewdly viewed by both writers as preeminently educative in the sense that its pursuit profoundly affects men's character, expectations, and beliefs.[102]

This assessment of Proudhon's interpretation of history shows it to be less defensible than its author thinks. But it also suggests that his view is less far-fetched than that of many of its rivals and that it contains several thought-provoking ideas. This may be a sufficient basis for concluding that it succeeds in plausibly explaining why the oppressive status quo need not be permanent.

If this conclusion is accepted, a new question immediately arises. Proudhon was not content to show that existing forms of oppression are impermanent; he also believed they should be abolished. Yet nothing in the explanatory part of his theory warrants this contention. Even proof far more positive than Proudhon's that liberation was possible would do nothing to support the proposition that it ought to occur. In order to prove this, an argument cast

[102] *Ibid.*, II, 198.

in moral terms is required. Proudhon had such an argument, which will be examined shortly. What must be said here is that his explanatory theory not only fails to support his commitment to total liberation, but actually undermines it. If Proudhon's psychological and sociological contentions are true, men must always be subject to restraints. But if some repression is unavoidable, then espousal of liberation, in any absolute sense, is futile. Thus, to the extent that Proudhon's awareness of the facts lays a realistic foundation for his ensuing attack on the existing world, it also sets up a barrier to a totally radical critique.

# CHAPTER III

## Dilemmas of Ethics

THE MOST perplexing thing about Proudhon's ethics is its ambivalence. This ambivalence comes out clearly in a short passage found in *Justice* dealing with the conflict between social convention and personal morality.[1] Proudhon considers a number of practices such as slavery, polygamy, and usury, all accepted in some societies and all wrong by his standards. He judges the decisions to follow these practices, the actions that accord with them, and the practices themselves. But it is impossible to tell what his final verdicts are.

Should one praise or blame a man who decides on grounds of moral principle to follow one of these practices? In one place Proudhon praises his decision: "A conscience that honestly subscribes to [such a practice] is justified." But the same decision is condemned a few pages later, where Proudhon writes that a popular but inadmissible practice "cannot go so far as to prevail against the moral sense, summoned unceasingly to reform it."

Are actions that accord with these practices right or wrong? Proudhon offers contradictory answers to this question. Acts forbidden by his moral standards "must always be condemned," he declares at one point. At another he says the opposite: "Conformity is just and devi-

[1] *Justice*, III, 355-61.

— 63 —

ance reprehensible," where established practices are concerned.

Finally, what about the merit of the practices themselves? Proudhon never says that they are laudable, since this would involve a blatant contradiction. Having expressed moral disapproval of slavery, polygamy, and usury, he cannot very well praise them. But he does vacillate between criticizing socially approved practices that are wrong by his standards, and treating them as morally irrelevant. He takes the second position when he writes, "From the point of view of Justice, slavery, warfare and usury are . . . trifles, polygamy is a trifle. . . . They are nothing but good or bad predicaments, accidents, hazards, errors of judgment if you like, but insignificant so far as morality is concerned." Yet Proudhon changes his mind two pages later by saying that conscience rightly declares practices like these to be "absurd and odious."

All these waverings are symptoms of indecision regarding two quite different ethical attitudes. Sometimes Proudhon opts for pure tolerance; he refuses to condemn decisions, conduct, and practices even though he disapproves of them. If others think and behave as seems good to them, he will not criticize. At other times he opts for strict rebuke of the choices, actions, and usages he thinks morally wrong. When he takes this tack, he denounces precisely what he accepts or even praises in his more tolerant moments.

There seems to be an explanation for Proudhon's wavering in the passage under consideration. He is careful to defend practices like slavery only where they are generally accepted. He will not tolerate slavery in a society that disapproves of it. This qualification suggests that what appears to be fluctuation between tolerance and severity is really adherence to the principle of cultural relativism.

Unfortunately, this explanation for his ambivalence does not hold water. For one thing, Proudhon's cultural relativism deserts him when he is judging action and choice. He has no qualms about condemning conduct and decisions that are generally approved. Even when he is discussing practices, he is not always a relativist. It is true that he never *defends* an unpopular practice, but he sometimes *attacks* one that is popular. He condemns punishing poor criminals more severely than rich ones, for example, even though this practice was quite widely accepted in his time.[2]

Since Proudhon's relativism is anything but consistent, it cannot account for his wavering. Close analysis of his ethical theory is needed. His fluctuations are signs of a more basic, though not fully explicit, tension in his moral thought.

### The Theoretical Roots of Proudhon's Ethical Ambivalence

One factor helping to explain Proudhon's vacillations between severity and tolerance is his view of how to make affirmations of intrinsic goodness. In his early writings his position on this basic issue of moral epistemology was confused, to say the least. Much evidence of naturalism can be found there, for Proudhon often said that ultimate

[2] Ch. Perelman analyzes this argument of Proudhon's in *The Idea of Justice and the Problem of Argument* (London, 1963), pp. 49-54.

values could be deduced from the state of public opinion, from examination of historical trends, or, more generally, from the nature of things. But mingled with this naturalism are statements of the intuitionist view that he eventually adopted. By the time he wrote *Justice*, his position was that affirmations of intrinsic goodness are made with the same sort of a priori intuition used to apprehend the truth of geometric axioms.[3]

It is easy to see why this view of ultimate ethical cognition nurtures his ambivalence. If knowledge of moral principles and geometric axioms are obtained in the same way, it is just as impossible to convince a man that his ethical convictions are wrong as to show him his mistake in thinking that parallel lines meet. A person subscribing to Proudhon's ethical epistemology, or Euclid's geometry, has only two choices when someone disagrees with him about basic axioms. He can adopt a strategy of tolerant non-intervention or of crusading imperialism. In other words, he can accept the fact of ultimate disagreement, or he can try to force his adversary to accept his own opinions. A third choice, discussion on merits, is not open to him, because his view of how ultimates are apprehended has foreclosed it.

Another aspect of Proudhon's theory of moral knowledge that helps explain his wavering is his view of how particular obligations are derived from ultimate norms. His position on this matter is deontological. He sees the relationship between particular duties and intrinsic values

---

[3] "There are things that I judge good and praiseworthy a priori, even though I do not yet have a clear idea of them; . . . and I approve of these things." *Justice*, III, 340.

as that of species to genus, not means to end. An action is right, he maintains, only if it conforms to the specifications of an ultimate norm, and regardless of the actual or expectable results that follow from adhering to it. Hence an intrinsically good action, such as telling the truth, "is indispensable, imperative, often onerous, indifferent to self-interest, concerned only with what is right and binding, however unprofitable circumstances make the former, however disastrous they make the latter."[4] This is but a version of the old saying, "*fiat justitia pereat mundus.*"

At first glance such a view seems severe. A deontologist like Proudhon, who eschews casuistry and derives specific duties directly from first principles, is able to praise and blame with extraordinary rigor. But there is also an implication in this viewpoint favorable to tolerance. Pure deontology leaves such a wide gap between general norms and detailed judgments that it weakens the reliability and the credibility of the moralist's verdicts. Insofar as he realizes this, he may be drawn toward toleration.

Still another element in Proudhon's moral thought that contributes to his ambivalence in his position on the issue of authority in moral matters. He insists that the last word in ethical disputes belongs to the adversaries themselves. Every man should decide for himself, at least about the specific obligations entailed by first principles. "In the last analysis, each individual is the judge of right and wrong and is empowered to act as an authority over himself and all others. If I decide for myself that something is unjust, it is futile for the prince or the priest to call it just and order me to do it: it remains unjust and im-

[4] *Ibid.*, I, 311.

moral. . . . And, conversely, if I decide inwardly that something is just, it is futile for the prince or the priest to claim to forbid me to do it: it remains just and moral."[5] This doctrine of inner light further reduces the persuasive power of Proudhon's ethics. If your conscience says some act or statement is wrong and his that it is right, there is little he can say to make you change your mind, since he acknowledges your own conscience as the best possible argument.

But the part of Proudhon's moral theory that helps more than any other to explain his shifts between restraint and activism is his choice of things worthwhile in themselves. His view is that only one thing has inherent value: respect, or, as he more frequently says, Justice.[6] By assigning inherent value to a single good, Proudhon nurtured his ambivalence in a way that is easily grasped. A man who thinks there is only one intrinsic good can judge more harshly than a man who thinks there are many. For him, moral judgment is cut-and-dried. But the very simple-mindedness of his verdicts may also incline him toward forebearance, if he is aware of it, for he will then see that his judgments are too unqualified.

The substance of Proudhon's highest good, as well as its form, does much to explain his wavering, for respect as he conceives it is very ambivalent. Proudhonian respect

[5] *Ibid.*, 1, 326; cf. 1v, 350.

[6] I will always refer to his highest value as "respect," however, since the conventional meaning of "justice" is so different from his own. For an excellent analysis of the relationship beween justice and respect see W. G. MacLagan, "Respect for Persons as a Moral Principle," *Philosophy*, xxxv, No. 134 (July 1960), pp. 193-204.

is first and foremost a state of mind. It is a disposition to view others "abstracted from their abilities, their contributions, their failures," i.e., apart from conventional standards of appraisal.[7] It means considering other people from their own point of view "simply as moral beings."[8] In short, respect means identifying with others, accepting their purposes and choices, empathizing with them.

Respect for Proudhon is more than a state of mind; it is a pattern of behavior too. To respect another is not only to identify with him, to mentally affirm his dignity, as Proudhon likes to say, but is also "to energetically defend that dignity, even at cost to oneself."[9] One must go beyond passively accepting the aims of others to actively protecting their freedom to pursue them.

Two inviolable moral rules are entailed by Proudhon's assignment of inherent value to respect as thus defined. The first enjoins us to accept the aims and decisions of others on their terms, as they understand them. The second binds us to defend the liberty of others to pursue their aims and carry out their choices. It prescribes freedom of action.

The second of these rules strengthens Proudhon's tendency toward forebearance, because it coincides with the obligation to be tolerant. A duty to defend the freedom of others to execute their decisions, whatever they may be, entails a duty to tolerate their actions. When a respecter is judging overt behavior, his obligation is therefore the same as a tolerator's. Both must allow others to do as they please.

[7] *Justice*, I, 301.    [8] *Ibid.*    [9] *Ibid.*, I, 414.

The first rule of respect—enjoining identification with the choices of others—makes Proudhon's ethic more severe than a morality of pure tolerance. A tolerant man may think what he likes about another's choice, provided that he allows him to carry it out. There is no place in his moral outlook for duties toward the decisions of other people. A respecting man, on the other hand, cannot be indifferent to conative states of mind. Unlike one who tolerates, he may not assume that it is "just and saintly" for a man "to satisfy . . . all his needs, all his whims," for one of his needs or whims may be to disregard or interfere with another man's decisions.[10] Instead he must "show intolerance [on] the issue of respect,"[11] by blocking decisions that disregard another's choices. Otherwise, men might not make the effort to accept their fellows' aims and choices—which is their highest duty. The conflict between the two basic rules of Proudhon's ethic thus introduces at its most fundamental level the same ambivalence that is found throughout.

### The Tasks of Moral Theory: Propagation and Application

It is one thing to show that Proudhon's shifts between severity and tolerance have roots deep in the structure of his moral theory and another to account for them in a satisfying way. The explanation offered so far is insufficient because it shows no more than that his vacillation was compatible with his moral view. It tells why Proudhon's theory *enabled* him to shuttle back and forth between these two attitudes, but not why it *impelled* him to.

[10] *Ibid.*, II, 96.    [11] *Ibid.*, III, 275; cf. I, 224-25.

This impulsion has its source in Proudhon's awareness of the problems raised by his ethics. Although nothing meant more to him than the triumph of respect, he saw numerous obstacles to this goal, and tried persistently to surmount them. One obstruction he considers is ethical ignorance. If men existed who could believe in no intrinsic goods at all, then Proudhon's ethic might collapse at its foundation. Such persons would be unable to accept any ethical norms whatever, including, of course, the rules of respect. Proudhon has two defenses against this hazard.

The first, based on reasoning by analogy from Descartes' *cogito ergo sum,* claims that the same argument which proves that people have personal identity also shows that they must believe in moral ultimates. This argument is certainly specious.

Descartes was able to refute the doubter of personal existence by showing that a precondition to his doubt was thought and that thinking in turn supposed personal existence. The *cogito* has force because its premise must be accepted by anyone who challenges it. Proudhon tries to turn this argument against the moral skeptic, the man who disclaims all capacity for belief in ethical ultimates. He seems to think that denial of a sense of right and wrong presupposes an exercise of conscience analogous to the use of reason to deny Descartes' *cogito.* "When you object that by myself I am unable to distinguish good from evil, . . . you implicitly assume that I have a sense or an idea of them."[12] This objection assumes no such

[12] *Ibid.,* III, 341.

thing. I cannot deny that I exist without making a factual judgment; but I can perfectly well deny my ability to believe in ultimate values without making an ethical one. No argument of the *cogito* type can work in the sphere of morals, because moral judgments are not purely cognitive.

Fortunately, Proudhon has a better answer to those who would deny a capacity for belief in moral ultimates. He admits that ethically ignorant persons exist, but points out that it is improper to regard them as moral beings. Proudhon says in effect that having a morality means at least believing some things are intrinsically valuable and approving of them. It follows that a person who does not have such beliefs and feelings lacks a morality and, like animals and other amoral beings, is not a fitting object of ethical concern.[18] This argument makes good sense. It is impossible to discuss moral questions with a man who thinks nothing is intrinsically worthwhile, because such a person cannot be convinced that an action or statement is morally good or bad. In order to make an ethical judgment one must have some basic standard of evaluation. A man who lacks such a standard is simply beyond the pale of moral discourse.

Proudhon's neat removal of ethical ignorance from the path to the supremacy of respect merely exposes a more serious obstacle. This is the danger of ethical disagreement. The problem here, to begin with, is that even moral persons may not accept respect as their highest value. *Justice* describes such a situation in the most ominous terms. It

[18] *Ibid.*, I, 296, 313; II, 344.

is nothing less than a "défaillance," which "seizes hold of
...society, invades men's minds, paralyzes liberty, dignity,
all the noble sentiments, and dooms entire peoples to
putrefaction."[14] Fear of this danger makes Proudhon seek
universal propagation of his first principles. He sees that if
the rules of respect are to reign supreme, they must be
placed uppermost in every man's conscience.

But even if everyone concurred on the intrinsic value of
respect, ethical disagreement could still block realization
of Proudhon's morality. While agreeing with him on
first principles, people might still reach different conclusions about the specific obligations entailed by them.

The peculiarities of the rules of respect make this prob
lem especially hard to solve. For one thing, their extreme
generality makes it hard to apply them to specific cases.
Hence the chance is slight that all who accept them will
apply them in the same way. Another difficulty in applying the rules of respect stems from their incompatibility.
The second rule enjoins leaving people free to pursue their
aims. Yet men who are free to work for all their purposes
may disobey the first rule of respect by failing to identify
with the decisions of others. The more faithfully the second rule is followed, the more likely the first will be violated. As Proudhon puts it, freedom of action is not only
an ingredient of respect, but is also "a force capable of
defeating it."[15]

Recognition of this danger leads him to put binding
application of his values as high on his agenda as their
universal propagation.[16] Fearing that people will not all

---

[14] *Ibid.*, III, 515.    [15] *Ibid.*, III, 518.

[16] "It is not enough to show the superiority of a theory; it is

apply his norms in the same way, he finds need for "a principle that acts on the will like a force and makes it choose the right course."[17] His attempts to both propagate and apply the rules of respect lead directly to the waverings in his moral outlook that we are trying to understand.

## False Solutions and Further Problems

Proudhon could have tried to carry out these tasks in many different ways, and it is to his credit that he considered and rejected some that have been chosen by thinkers of greater stature.

For the job of propagating respect, he rejects a number of candidates, such as religion, science, and government, that might diffuse his values by authoritative decree. His arguments against using religion in this way are the same as those he uses against the others, and may be treated as paradigmatic.

The first argument against religion points out that one cannot draw ethical conclusions from purely religious premises, about God's will or commands. "The concept of religion can be deduced: that is what theology does. The concept of Justice can also be deduced. . . . But Justice and its laws cannot be logically deduced from the concept of religion, nor can religion and its dogmas be linked to the juridical concept: they are two totally distinct classes of ideas."[18] Put in more contemporary idiom, Proudhon is saying that theological statements, being in the in-

---

also necessary to assure . . . that it does not fail miserably in the face of difficulties of application." *Ibid.*, 1, 306.

[17] *Ibid.*, 1, 315.     [18] *Ibid.*, 1, 365.

dicative mood, cannot by themselves validate ethical statements that are cast in the imperative.

Proudhon is not content with a metaethical denial of the power of religion to disseminate his values. He wants to show that it would be bad to use religion for this purpose, even if it were logically possible to do so. This he does by pointing to the conflict between respect's imperatives and the duty to obey divine commands. A Proudhonian ethic, with its commitment to the autonomy of individual conscience, requires me to follow every moral rule, and, a fortiori, the rules of respect, because I think I should, not because an external agent like God wants me to. "The intervention of a supernatural authority . . . is destructive to Justice. . . . Justice must be independently affirmed and defended, or it does not exist."[19]

By using these arguments to repudiate all higher authorities, not just religion, Proudhon increased the consistency of his position, because he thereby excluded resort to devices for diffusing his values that are incompatible with them. But he also intensified the problem of their dissemination. For if subjection to the sway of authorities like religion, government, and science is impermissible, what could induce men to adopt respect as their basic moral principle?

He faced the same dilemma when he examined candidates that might help apply his morality to particular cases. Altruism, for instance, might help in this task, for if people were altruistic, they would seldom violate the rules of respect by ignoring the aims of others or block-

[19] *Ibid.*, I, 449.

ing their actions. Rather, they would go out of their way to help others reach their objectives.

Proudhon's psychology keeps him from accepting this line of argument, for it denies the actual or potential force of altruistic motives. Another reason for his rejection of altruism is based on ethical considerations. This argument questions not its psychological force, but its moral authority. Altruism is "an instinctive feeling, which it is useful and laudable to cultivate, but which, far from engendering respect and dignity, is strictly incompatible with them."[20] In short, there is a conflict between the practice of benevolence and the obligations of respect. Altruism, as a form of love, "cannot be willed." And since "we are not free to love," we can have no obligation to.[21] Moreover, while respect enjoins allowing people to do what they please, it imposes no duty to help them. In fact, respect requires dispensing with help. "The essence of our dignity is to do without the aid of others."[22] Since I act disrespectfully toward my neighbor when I help him as well as when I hinder him, I have an obligation to avoid both.

Another force considered by Proudhon as an aid to applying his morality is compatible egoism, the disposition to find self-satisfaction in ends harmonious with those that others seek. If people always pursued self-regarding ends, and if such ends were compatible, it would be easy for them to follow at least the second rule of respect. For they would never interfere with the efforts of others toward goal attainment, no matter what they did. Proudhon re-

[20] *Ibid.*, I, 416; cf. III, 516.   [21] *Ibid.*, I, 350, 427.
[22] *Ibid.*, I, 417.

buts the case for compatible egoism by examining its assumptions. In the first place, people do not always pursue self-regarding ends. They occasionally follow their consciences or their generous impulses when these conflict with their selfish ones.[23] When this happens, compatible egoism is of no use, even if it exists, because then behavior is not motivated by egoism at all. More important is the point that egoistic action is *not* always compatible with the goal attainment of others. "Because of their mobile and evolving character, interests . . . continually block one another."[24] The case for compatible egoism is thus "reduced to a *petitio principii*. It takes for granted what can never be achieved."[25]

Compelling moral knowledge is the last force considered by Proudhon as a possible aid to applying respect. If moral knowledge compelled right conduct, those who knew the rules of respect would necessarily follow them. No problem of application would arise, because all who accepted them would use them correctly. According to Proudhon, the psychological facts refute this contention too. Conscience is very weak; hence there can be no guarantee that men with moral knowledge will act accordingly. In fact, they will do the opposite of what they think right, in most cases. Moreover, even if moral knowledge *were* compelling, it would not alleviate the danger of ethical disagreement very much. Moral, as opposed to factual, knowledge is difficult to obtain. It "must be continually amended, as indicated by the experiences of daily life."[26] Since few true statements can be made on

---

[23] *Ibid.*, I, 310.     [24] *Ibid.*, I, 301.     [25] *Ibid.*
[26] *Ibid.*, I, 304.

moral issues, knowledge can seldom arbitrate ethical disputes.

By rejecting all these forces as aids to the application of respect, Proudhon of course made the job of applying it more difficult. Just as his refusal to invoke higher authorities made it hard for him to win universal acceptance for the rules of respect, so his unwillingness to rely on altruism, compatible egoism, or compelling knowledge complicated the problem of assuring that men applied these rules correctly to their daily lives.

## Social Pressure

Proudhon usually tries to solve both of these problems by offering proof that respect is the ultimate criterion of value. He seems to think that if only he can show the supremacy of the rules of respect, they will be automatically accepted and applied. This solution has two shortcomings. In the first place, it is no more compatible with Proudhon's psychology than any of the solutions he rejects. No matter how cogent his proof of respect's goodness, he cannot hope to succeed in diffusing and applying respect, because his psychology warns that people convinced of its value will not necessarily act accordingly. Even more damaging is the logical impossibility of adducing such proof. No norm can be proved supreme, because such proof would entail testing that norm with another one. But in that case, the norm used as a criterion of value, and not the one being tested, would have to be regarded as supreme. Hence Proudhon cannot refute those who deny the supremacy of respect without dethroning it from its position as the highest good.

Since the method most frequently relied on by Proudhon to solve the problems raised by his ethics cannot possibly succeed, there seems no escape from the conclusion that his moral theory is a failure on its own terms. But before we draw this conclusion, one more point must be considered. In one place in his published writings, at the very end of *Justice*, Proudhon suggests a vastly different method for diffusing and applying respect. What he says then is that "society" should "use the powerful stimuli of collective conscience to develop the moral sense of all its members."[27] Here Proudhon espouses ethical conventionalism, the doctrine that people should obey the dictates of public opinion. He assumes that men who feel bound to obey the informal social pressures they exert on one another will be sure to accept and follow the rules of respect.

*Justice* offers no defense of this position. Its espousal of conventionalism is not connected with the rest of its moral theory—except by fiat. For over a thousand pages nothing is said about a duty to obey public opinion.[28] Then, it suddenly appears as a *deus ex machina,* to end what was threatening to become an interminable search.

One is tempted to say that Proudhon committed more than a non sequitur by preaching conventionalism at the

[27] *Justice,* IV, 368; cf. IV, 366.

[28] It is true that there are hints of moral conventionalism in earlier parts of the book, e.g., "In the last resort, each judges . . . himself *and all others,*" I, 326 (my italics); or, "men . . . are one another's guarantors," I, 419. But these phrases are so vague that it would be impossible to see them as enjoining obedience to social pressure, were it not for the frank prescription of this duty at the book's very end.

last minute. Did he not also introduce a blatant contradiction into the heart of his system? After ostentatiously rejecting all authoritarian sanctions for morality as incompatible with the autonomous conduct demanded by respect, he seems to have inconspicuously admitted one, in the guise of social pressure. Proudhon realized that this accusation has great weight. "After destroying that double conscience in us, for which we so strongly condemned religion, will we recreate it by means of this collective conscience, whose prescriptions have such trouble penetrating individual minds? Won't this structure lead us into new hypocrisy, rather than assuring social trust?"[29] An analysis of his defense against this charge is illuminating; it exposes another layer of theoretical confusion.

Proudhon tries to cleanse social pressure of the taint of disrespect by contrasting its origin with that of the authorities he disapproves. All of these, be they the decrees of God, rulers, or the spokesmen of science, are an imposed "pressure from without, exerted on the self."[30] Social pressure, on the other hand, does not restrain from outside. Its influence "would never be transformed into an obligatory law for the will without an emotional predisposition which makes the social relations that embrace the subject appear to him as . . . a sort of secret commandment from himself to himself."[31] His point here is that since social authority, unlike other authority, is an informal force, lacking explicit promulgators and sanctions, it cannot operate unless its imperatives are internalized by those at whom it is directed. The implication of this con-

[29] *Justice*, III, 263-64.      [30] *Ibid.*, I, 316.
[31] *Ibid.*, I, 325.

trast is that social pressure, being self-imposed, does not interfere externally with action and choice, and so is not disrespectful.[32]

This conclusion is of course fallacious and conflicts with Proudhon's whole moral viewpoint. To begin with, its premise is mistaken, since it is not true that social authority works only if internalized. It may also control externally, with sanctions that range from mild stigma to complete ostracism. Insofar as it restrains in this way, social pressure shares the faults that Proudhon finds in political, religious, and scientific authority.

But even if the premise of this argument were correct, and social pressure could control only when internalized, a duty to obey it would still contradict Proudhon's highest value. Respect demands that I be free to choose and act as I see fit, unimpeded by the will of any other man. The pressures of society, for all their spontaneity and impersonality, are nonetheless interferences of external human origin, and rather strong ones at that. Even if they must be internalized to be effective, this does not prevent them from constraining, because the process of internalization may itself involve external coercion. Proudhon saw this perfectly when considering inward assent to political and religious authority. If I internalize religious norms, for instance, I may be unwittingly coerced by "Another, namely God, . . . who directs me, without my knowing it, by His

[32] In the "Cours" at I 3 (2), Proudhon goes even further, by saying that social pressure increases freedom. "Society does not limit men . . . it instructs them, i.e., it *arms* them and *emancipates* them: by making them cooperate for a common end, it gives them independence."

imperious suggestion, just when I imagine I am acting autonomously by following the moral law."[33] There is really no significant difference if the "other" is society.[34]

The explanation for Proudhon's failure to identify the disrespectful origin of social pressure is rather obvious. Had he called attention to how public opinion interferes with action and choice, he would have had to admit that it was a no more suitable moralizer than the other authorities. But such an admission would have put an end to his ethical theorizing. Having ruled out all other methods for diffusing and applying his morality, he had to salvage the remaining one as best he could, even if this meant resorting to unfounded distinctions.

Suppose nonetheless, for the sake of argument, that Proudhon is correct in saying that social authority is not disrespectful in origin. Even then conventionalism poses a serious problem. How can I reconcile my obligation to obey social pressure with my duty to follow the rules of respect when the two conflict, as they will when others fail to identify with decisions or block their execution? Unless Proudhon says that I should disregard public opinion when it violates the rules of respect, he tacitly justifies my submission to pressures that may perhaps not be disrespectful in origin, but certainly are disrespectful

[33] *Justice*, I, 322-23.

[34] The much maligned Arthur Desjardins seems to be the only critic who noticed this. His conservatism often distorted his analysis of Proudhon's position, but he did see that by advocating social pressure Proudhon contradicted himself: "You subject men to such discipline and yet you think you have suppressed government!" *Proudhon, sa vie, ses oeuvres, sa doctrine* (Paris, 1896), II, 203.

in content. For then I must follow convention, whatever it decrees, even if it ignores aims and interferes with conduct.

But to accuse Proudhon of contradicting himself in this way would be to say too much. He would have made this mistake only if he had claimed that public opinion is always right and hence should always be obeyed. This he never did. In fact, though he never went so far as to condemn disrespectful social pressure, he did say that in certain unspecified cases it could be rightfully ignored.[35] Though he thereby escaped the accusation of inconsistency, he left himself open to the only slightly less serious reproach of evading a crucial problem connected with conventionalism. To assert dogmatically that social authority should sometimes but not always be obeyed tells nothing of significance to a person who needs moral guidance in a particular situation. And this, ostensibly, is the sort of advice Proudhon intends to give.

His solution to his basic ethical problem is thus subject to three criticisms. (1) It is not logically connected with the rest of his moral theory, but is a crutch, added at the end, instead of one of the vital organs of the system. (2) It is an unsuitable crutch because it is repugnant to the first principles of the system. (3) It fails to offer the specific guidance it is supposed to furnish.

The odd discontinuity in Proudhon's ethics and the surprising severity of its suggested moralizing force have provoked extended controversy between commentators who call him a "moralist" and those who see him as a "sociologist." The former stress the heart of his theory—

[35] *Justice*, IV, 487.

the rules of respect—and disregard what comes after the non sequitur—its conventionalism. Or, put another way, they take his vague assertion that social authority is sometimes wrong to mean that it frequently is, and that individuals are then justified in ignoring it. Elie Halévy gave classic form to this interpretation at a meeting of the Société française de philosophie held in 1912, where this issue was first publicly discussed. According to Halévy, Proudhon believes that each individual should obey his own conscience when it conflicts with convention. "Where Proudhon presents the principles of his ethics most didactically—in the first chapters of *Justice*—he makes not the slightest allusion to an alleged social origin of reason's commands."[36]

The "sociologist" interpretation was advanced in the same discussion by Célestin Bouglé. He emphasized Proudhon's moral conventionalism and narrowly construed his warning that public opinion may be mistaken to mean that it hardly ever is. By doing so, he was able to say that Proudhon subordinates conscience to convention, by making moral obligation "a revelation of the Collective."[37]

This debate set the terms for much subsequent controversy about Proudhon's ethics. Even today commentators sometimes feel the need to choose between Proudhon the "moralist" and Proudhon the "sociologist."[38] Yet such a choice is pointless, for there is evidence to support, and

[36] *Bulletin de la société française de philosophie*, XII (Paris, 1912), p. 191.

[37] *Ibid.*, p. 170.

[38] Among the followers of the "sociologist" line are Jeanne Duprat and Georges Gurvitch. Georges Guy-Grand is on the "moralist" side.

refute, both alternatives. Fortunately, material in the un-published "Cours" shows a way out of what has by now become a rather arid interpretational impasse.

## *Vigilante Justice*

The sections on morality in the "Cours" fill some of the gaps in Proudhon's definitive work on ethics and remove some of its ambiguities. To begin with, the "Cours" supplies the justification for ethical conventionalism missing from *Justice*. It states unequivocally that any infringement of "the rights of society" is a threat to collective survival. Moreover, the only way to secure these rights is by giving them precedence over the rights of individuals. In Prou-dhon's words, "the individual conscience must be taught to identify with the social conscience" for the sake of social survival.[39]

Though the "Cours" justifies conventional morality more explicitly than *Justice*, it does not go so far as to say that convention is always right. Like *Justice*, but with greater forthrightness, it too denies convention's infalli-bility. "In the ordinary practices of individual life, the Collective Being must be considered supremely immor-al."[40] The "Cours" then carries out the job that *Justice* shirks. It suggests a way to judge and control the dictates of social pressure. What it prescribes is recourse to vigi-lante justice. A privately organized band of righteous men is to make public opinion accord with the rules of respect by coercively enforcing compliance with them.

The "Cours" is not the only place where Proudhon

[39] "Cours," I-10 (8); cf. *ibid.*, I-14A (11).
[40] *Ibid.*, I-10 (7).

praises vigilanteism; but all of his other favorable references to it, like this one, are in unpublished papers and letters. His earliest support for it is in a letter written to explain a cryptic reference in the *Avertissement aux propriétaires* to a moralizing method "which is known, but cannot be mentioned."[41] This method turns out to be a secret society of "justiciers," modelled after the medieval Germanic *Vehmgerichte*, whose job is to punish all cases of immoral conduct and suppress every immoral thought.[42] The theme of vigilanteism also appears now and then in the *Carnets*. They recommend private execution of the wicked, summary punishment of a long list of evil doings like treason and adultery, and formation of a band of zealots, a "sainte Vehme," to end corruption.[43] Such outbursts occur in early, middle, and late *Carnets*; they are a permanent but repressed part of Proudhon's thought.

The "Cours" goes beyond mere praise of vigilante justice by giving it a specific role to play. Suppose that prevailing sentiment and behavior are disrespectful and that "only a few bands of puritans still protest: Have they the right to?" Indeed they do, no matter how small their number. Even if "an entire people prevaricated, I would still have the right to protest, and, if not to avenge justice, at least be its martyr."[44] The vigilance of a morally pure elite here becomes the ultimate recourse for judging social authority and for controlling it.

[41] *Avert.*, p. 247.
[42] *Lettres à Chaudey et à divers Comtois*, ed. Edouard Droz (Besançon, 1911), p. 83.
[43] *Carnets*, VI, 100; IX, 176; XI, 505.
[44] "Cours," I-14D' (71).

By preaching vigilanteism, the "Cours" frees Proudhon's ethics of the wavering between personal and conventional morality that encumbers his published writings. This makes it possible to settle the dispute between "moralist" and "sociologist" interpretations, so far as the "Cours" is concerned. In that work, Proudhon resolves his indecision between conscience and convention by distinguishing an elite of *justiciers* who are to follow their own principles and an impure mass which is to follow public opinion, as shaped by the elite. The "Cours" makes Proudhon a "moralist" with respect to the elite, and a "sociologist" with respect to the mass.

Unfortunately, this resolution of Proudhon's ambivalence cannot be applied to his published writings, for he suppressed all favorable references to vigilanteism when he committed himself publicly on ethical matters. But though the "Cours" cannot settle the old dispute between "moralist" and "sociologist" views of Proudhonian morality, it can do something at least as worthwhile, by suggesting a change in the central question of interpretation raised by his ethics. Rather than trying to decide if Proudhon is really for conscience or for convention, we may now ask why he thought it necessary to rely on both, and why he evaded the problem of reconciling them, even though he had once privately suggested a way to do so.

In *Justice*, Proudhon explains why he finally decided not to recommend vigilante justice. He remains convinced that in principle it is a good way to enforce right attitudes and behavior, because vigilantes follow their own consciences in carrying out their job, not the authority of an external agent. He continues to uphold vigilanteism as a highly effective method for regulating conduct. But he also recognizes that it faces grave practical difficulties. It would be very hard to assure that the hundred or so puritans, who are to abolish every evil thought and deed, limit their persecution to cases of genuine disrespect. And if they tried to restrict themselves to such cases, the vigilantes would probably be insufficiently vigorous in their persecution. Vigilante justice is likely to degenerate into a reign of terror or a comedy of pious moralizing. In sum, although a vigilance committee to serve as "the true organ and worthy avenger of the social conscience" appeals to Proudhon because of its moralizing promise, he finally has to admit, as a consistent realist, that it is "the most unrealizable of utopias."[45]

Having rejected vigilante justice, he revised his estimate of social pressure. The "Cours" said that public opinion checked by vigilantes is supremely virtuous. But once vigilante justice was declared unreliable, the force it was supposed to check seemed dangerous too. *Justice* therefore takes an indecisive view. There are passages that justify obedience to social pressure; others criticize it. Proudhon even complains that if convention is accepted as morally binding, society, "exterior and superior to the individual, enjoys the sole initiative; outside of it there is no free action; everything is absorbed in an anonymous, aristocratic, unquestionable authority."[46]

---

[45] *Justice*, iv, 465.
[46] *Ibid.*, i, 303; cf. iv, 363: "It is contrary to all philosophy, after having recognized an *internal* sanction, to speak of an *external* sanction, whose administrator would be God, the Church or society." The parallel treatment of social and religious sanctions in this text is remarkable, since Proudhon carefully distinguishes them elsewhere in the same book.

This indecision shows that at the end of his journey Proudhon had not reached his destination. He had been looking for a way to diffuse and apply a system of ethics both abstract and ambiguous. For a while, obligatory social pressure checked by vigilanteism seemed to be the answer. But second thoughts convinced him that this means for checking convention was too perilous to recommend. One might expect him to acknowledge defeat and end his search. This he was not prepared to do. Instead, he held fast to all the unreconciled elements in his morality and evaded the task of bringing them together.[47]

The troubles caused Proudhon by the conflict between conscience and convention suggest a fuller explanation for his wavering between severity and tolerance. Their opposed claims place him in an awkward position when faced by a problem like judging a slaveowner in a society that approves slavery. Considered from one angle, the claims of conscience call for tolerating, or even condoning, the slaveowner's aim and action. Respect demands

[47] Pierre Haubtmann is the only other writer who has used evidence from the "Cours" to illuminate Proudhon's ambivalence between conscience and convention. See his thesis, "La philosophie sociale de Proudhon," (Faculté des lettres et des sciences humaines de Paris, 1961) chs. 4,6. He agrees that while there is more ethical conventionalism in the "Cours" than in *Justice*, some can be found in both; and that while personal morality is stressed more in *Justice*, it is not completely ignored by the "Cours." Nevertheless, Haubtmann goes further than is warranted by the texts toward portraying Proudhon as a "sociologist" in the "Cours" and a "moralist" in *Justice*. Part of the reason for this distortion may be Haubtmann's failure to consider the bearing of vigilante justice on Proudhon's waverings. The "Cours'" defense of vigilanteism makes it a weaker partisan of convention than would be true otherwise, while *Justice*'s eschewal of vigilanteism makes that work more favorable to convention than would otherwise be the case.

that one identify with the purposes of another and defend his pursuit of them. One should not interfere with the slaveowner, especially in a society where slavery is accepted, where the slaves themselves are unlikely to think they are being treated disrespectfully. The claims of conventional morality reinforce the duty to tolerate the slaveowner; after all, he is doing the accepted thing in keeping slaves, and adherence to public opinion is desirable.

On the other hand, Proudhon's theory also makes a strong case for criticizing the slaveowner. Conscience enjoins us to understand the purpose of other men, yet the slaveowner always disregards and sometimes thwarts his slaves' aims. As for convention, it ought to be observed only when it promotes respect, and it is very doubtful that social pressure favorable to slaveholding does so. When Proudhon considers these implications of his viewpoint, he naturally tends to criticize the slaveowner, and since he has no principle for adjudicating between the conflicting claims of his morality, he has no way to choose between them.

### Kantian Formalism and Proudhonian Practicality

Although Proudhon does not admit it, his moral outlook is more like Kant's than that of any other theorist's. Comparison of the two should therefore bring out the character of Proudhon's ethics more clearly than has been possible thus far.

Both writers take the same position on the important metaethical questions. They both opt for a priori intuitionism, deontology, and the supremacy of the autonomous conscience. The main lines of their normative ethics are also similar. When expressed as the rule that one should always treat others as ends in themselves, never as means only, Kant's categorical imperative has a meaning very like Proudhon's rules of respect. Both enjoin us to acknowledge the legitimacy of the purposes of others and to avoid interfering with their actions. But Proudhon's theory diverges from that of his predecessor in two revealing ways.

First, though Proudhon accepts Kant's picture of moral perfection, he wants to apply it more concretely, by deriving from it detailed imperative advice. The trouble with the categorical imperative, he writes, is "that instead of defining Justice, it raises a question about it. . . . How can I know whether or not my action can serve as a general rule?"[48] This vagueness will not do. The moral law must be "decreed for every level of civilization and all possible cases."[49]

Proudhon also differs from Kant by applying their shared picture of moral perfection to a wider range of conduct. Kant recognized that not everyone would follow, or even accept, the categorical imperative. He therefore relied on legal as well as moral rules to regulate behavior. In that sphere of action where one man can reduce another's liberty, law was to protect the freedom of the individual to pursue his goals, so that he could reach them even if others ignored their moral duty to let him do so.[50] Proudhon, on the other hand, thought respect could be so widely diffused that men would invariably

[48] *Justice*, I, 430.　　　　　　[49] *Ibid.*, III, 355.
[50] Immanuel Kant, *The Metaphysical Elements of Justice*, trans., John Ladd (Indianapolis, 1965), pp. 34-35.

acknowledge the legitimacy of the goals of others. Hence he saw no need to reinforce moral with juridical obligation and relied solely on the rules of respect to regulate behavior.[51] His version of the categorical imperative thus has a wider scope than Kant's: it is the sole directing agent for all aspects of men's lives.

The extensions of Kantian ethics sought by Proudhon through particularizing its application and broadening its scope are surely impossible to achieve. A deontological ethic of principle cannot furnish wide-ranging detailed advice, because it is the sort of ethic that gives little consideration to particular circumstances. The limits on Kant's morality, which so dissatisfy Proudhon, are imposed by the nature of its premises. Why then did Proudhon try to remove them? And why did his attempt launch him on such an arduous but inconclusive intellectual voyage? Reference to his radicalism and realism suggests answers.

Proudhon tried to remove Kant's limitations because they stood in the way of his radical impulses. In his eyes, respect is such a valuable good that one cannot be content with its partial attainment. Instead, one must strive incessantly for its perfect realization, no matter what the obstacles. This endeavor would not have led Proudhon down such a sinuous path, had he not been realistic; he would have been oblivious to most of the obstacles that blocked his way. It was only because he was a realist that he faced and tried to deal with so many of the theoretical problems raised by his enterprise.

Judged by its own pretensions, Proudhon's theory of

[51] *Justice,* IV, 368.

morals is a failure. But since its shortcomings spring from the convergence of radical zeal and realistic insight, its failure on its own terms by no means deprives it of all value. On the contrary, his attempt to reconcile an ardent desire for respect and freedom with appreciation of the difficulties involved makes his theory a useful model for understanding what happens when these two attitudes intersect. Perhaps its most important lesson is that since unlimited observance of respect's imperatives is unachievable, anyone who wants to extend personal liberty and increase the justice of human relations must admit that success will be limited, but he should not therefore renounce his effort to obtain it. By showing this, Proudhon set an example relevant for those whose dilemmas are evoked by his way of thinking.

# CHAPTER IV

# Proudhon as a Radical Critic of
# Established Institutions

CRITIC qualifies as radical by carrying his assault on the status quo beyond its surface defects to their hidden sources. He grabs matters by the root, as Marx said, while others are content to prune their leaves and branches. Proudhon wants to grab by the root what he regards as the present world's most potent instruments of oppression: hierarchy and government.[1]

## *The Social Evils: Deference and Inequality*

Proudhon's critique is usually examined from an economic angle. Most commentators have placed it in that long line of attacks on exploitation known as socialism. Yet this perspective obscures as much as it clarifies. For though Proudhon was indeed a vigorous opponent of exploitation, his strictures against it are an outgrowth of something more basic. He denounced exploitation because he saw in it the same disrespectful features that he condemned in other aspects of modern society. To fully understand the critical side of his theory it is therefore necessary to focus attention on its general premises, rather than on its application to economics.

---

[1] Proudhon, of course, believed that religion was a third instrument of oppression. This should not be forgotten but bears only indirectly on his social and political ideas.

Proudhon's opposition to existing social arrangements is inspired by Rousseau's similar onslaught in the *Discourse on Inequality*. Proudhon's only quarrel with Rousseau's critique is that it does not go far enough; his mistake "is not, cannot be in his negation of society: it consists . . . in his not having carried his argument to the end."[2] Proudhon proposes to resume Rousseau's battle and press on to a complete victory.[3] He accepts his forebear's critical premises and draws out their extreme conclusions.

Both writers make the same practice the target of their attack: deference, the use of conventional standards of rank—mainly wealth, power, and prestige—to rate all members of society.[4] In Rousseau's words, which could just as well have been Proudhon's, when "a value came to be attached to public esteem," so that men "set a value on the opinion of the rest of the world," the first step "toward vice" was taken and "combinations fatal to innocence and happiness" resulted.[5] Where Proudhon differs from Rousseau is in being more explicit about the

[2] *Cont.*, I, 351.

[3] "Rousseau has always struck me as misunderstanding the cause he wanted to defend and as getting entangled in baseless a priority, when he should have reasoned according to the nature of things." *Dim.*, p. 55.

[4] Jean-Jacques Rousseau, *The Social Contract and Discourses*, trans., G.D.H. Cole (New York, 1950), p. 265. Cf. *Justice*, III, 174: "Generally, the consideration attached to a man . . . is proportional to his reputation, his fortune and his power. We are so made that we always suppose that noumena are proportional to phenomena, that appearance is proportional to reality." The contrast between reality and appearance (*être* and *paraître*) was also much emphasized by Rousseau, e.g., p. 247.

[5] Rousseau, pp. 240-41, 270.

reasons why deference is bad. Unlike his forebear, he has precise norms with which to appraise it. Though he never formally judged deference by the rules of respect, his thought can be completed by considering the remarks he makes about it in the light of their critical implications.

The first rule of respect enjoins acceptance of the choices of others. A man who practices deference has little concern for the decisions made by those he ranks as poor, weak, and lowly. Thinking them unworthy of consideration, he tends to disregard their decisions, or perhaps impute false ones to them. Moreover, he will be just as mistaken about the aims of those he ranks highly. Thinking of them as strong, rich, or honored, he will tend to believe that they seek power, money, or prestige.

In the "Cours" Proudhon compares this deferential social outlook with the way an army's echelons regard one another. The soldier accepts military rank as his evaluative standard and hence tends to ignore the aims of his subordinates and misunderstand those of his superiors: it is not worthwhile to find out what the privates want, the generals' objective is obviously to command.[6] In society as a whole there is the same connection between judging others according to rank and misunderstanding their purposes. Choice can never be free where men view one another in a graded hierarchy.

Judged by the second rule of respect—enjoining freedom of action—deference appears as pernicious as when judged by the first. It is easily seen that one will be apt to hinder the execution of decisions which one misunderstands or denigrates. Hence, in a deferential society, the

[6] "Cours," I-3 (30).

poor, unhonored, and weak will usually be kept from reaching their ends, while those highly ranked in these respects are allowed to attain theirs. Deference engenders "special perquisites, privileges, exemptions, favors, exceptions, all the violations of justice"—in short, oppression, including economic exploitation of the unprivileged.[7]

If respect is impossible in a deferential society, how do its members treat one another? Those who enjoy high esteem can be said to respect others only "if by respect you mean the compliments, obeisances, and all the affectations of a puerile and Christian civility. Is it not the height of good breeding for a great lord to know how to say 'hello!' in as many different ways as there are rungs on the hierarchic ladder? M. Guizot calls this science of pretences respect. For us, men of the Revolution, it is insolence."[8] As for those who give deference, they are just as disrespectful as those who receive it. The only difference is that the highly esteemed are arrogant, while the lowly ranked are servile. To those at the bottom, with their "instinctive obedience," the rich, honored, and powerful "always seem to be thirty centimeters taller than other men."[9]

Having shown more fully than Rousseau why deference leads to injustice and oppression, Proudhon goes on to draw the critical conclusions his predecessor had avoided. The most obvious is that the practice of deference, being supremely immoral, ought to be abolished. Rousseau was kept from saying this by his belief that deference is due to social inequality.[10] By ascribing deference to this par-

---

[7] *Justice*, III, 174.  [8] *Ibid.*, II, 383.  [9] *Cap.*, p. 88.
[10] Rousseau, p. 271.

ticular cause, he made its cure depend on the creation of a strictly egalitarian society. But he doubted the possibility, and feared the consequences of such a society. Hence, though he deplored deference as much as Proudhon, he did not want to eliminate it. It was to be maintained and only its worst symptoms alleviated.[11]

Proudhon agrees completely with Rousseau about the cause of deference and, consequently, about what is needed to abolish it. Deference, he says, arises from "the distinction of ranks. . . . As long as [a] society includes a mean and extremes, the distance remains the same between the poor and the rich, between the serf and the baron; there is no public happiness."[12] But he disagrees with Rousseau about the possibility and value of eliminating hierarchy. Hence, while he praises his predecessor for ascribing deference to inequality, he berates him for "relegating equality to the status of an ideal."[13] Such equivocation is inadmissible. Since inequality causes deference, and since deference is profoundly objectionable, inequality must be abolished.[14]

Proudhon even goes a step further. The existence of inequality presupposes application of a rule that tells how

[11] Judith Shklar, "Rousseau's Images of Authority," *American Political Science Review*, LVIII, No. 4 (December 1964), p. 920.

[12] *Avert.*, pp. 205-206.

[13] Quoted in Pierre Haubtmann, "Pierre-Joseph Proudhon: sa vie et sa pensée" (unpublished thesis for the Doctorat d'Etat, Faculté des lettres et des sciences humaines de Paris, 1961), p. 282, annex 20.

[14] Proudhon also condemns hierarchy for causing political oppression. This aspect of his social criticism is discussed in the next section of this chapter, where his critique of government is examined.

much wealth, power, and prestige each member of society should receive. Such a rule, indicating how goods should be allocated among members of society, is an obvious example of a principle of distributive justice. Hence, if inequality is to be abolished so must its underlying distributive principle. All rules of distributive justice must be eliminated.[15]

By assailing the venerable distributive principle, Proudhon introduced a radical element into his critique. Condemnation of hierarchy was itself a radical move, since hierarchy is a basic feature of all existing societies. But criticism of distributive justice went even further. For no thinker, however libertarian, had ever dared to question the view that some rules for allocating goods are indispensable for social life.

Proudhon's total opposition to distributive justice had curious results for his attitude toward those of his contemporaries who shared his hostility to inequality. Their view contrasted with his in that they did not oppose the principle of distributive justice, but simply wanted to apply it differently. Proudhon found himself objecting more strongly to these contemporaries than to the hierarchy that was their common enemy.

One kind of attack on inequality came from the liberals, who objected to the caste features of existing rank differences. What bothered them was that the prestige, power, or wealth a man enjoys is too often unrelated to the ef-

---

[15] *Prop.*, p. 313; *I.G.*, p. 187; *Justice*, I, 453. Yves Simon is the only critic, so far as I know, who remarks on Proudhon's total hostility to distributive justice. See his "Note sur le fédéralisme proudhonien," *Esprit*, No. 55 (April 1937), p. 55.

forts he makes to obtain it. Instead, it devolves on him by virtue of some circumstance beyond his control, such as his birth. In this view inequality is perfectly legitimate, provided it arises for the right reasons. Liberals do not find fault with the principle of distribution *per se*, but only with the way it is actually applied.

Proudhon attacked the liberals repeatedly, on the ground that they would merely substitute one form of inequality for another. One of their arguments, used in Proudhon's day by the Saint-Simonians, criticizes the existing hierarchy as unfair to the claims of talent. But, as Proudhon points out, the application of the principle, to each according to his ability, rules out "both the fact of equality and the right to it." A hierarchy of talent is still a hierarchy. Hence "the evaluation of talents . . . is an offense against personal dignity."[16] Another liberal attack on inequality objects to its inadequate compensation of productive contribution. Proudhon opposes this position too. "Is it just that he who does more receives more?" No indeed! "All workers are equal; . . . the product of each is limited by the right of all."[17]

The other prevalent objection to the existing pattern of inequality came from the socialists, who criticized, not its neglect of personal achievement, but its frustration of basic human needs. They felt the unequal distribution of advantages kept too many people from enjoying a decent standard of living. This criticism of inequality could be no more acceptable to Proudhon than the other. It too

[16] *Justice*, ii, 72.

[17] *Prop.*, pp. 221-22. Proudhon later reneged this criticism, as will become clear in due course.

finds nothing intrinsically wrong with ranking people and merely prescribes a different distributive rule. Hence Proudhon repeatedly attacks the two leading French spokesmen for this view, Louis Blanc and Etienne Cabet, who both defend the formula, to each according to his need. This maxim "accords less than equality: it preserves inequality."[18] Since needs vary, reward proportioned to them produces unequal distribution of income. The criterion of need must also cause substantial inequality of power. "Who will be the judge of need?" Each man cannot be his own judge, for unreconcilable disputes would arise. So decisions about needs "will be coercively enforced." But "that is slavery." Distribution according to need "leads to despotism."[19]

It is hard to see how Proudhon's attack on inequality could have been any more radical than this. His opposition is so fundamental that not one of its other critics is spared by his attack.[20]

## The Political Evils: Government and Law

Anyone acquainted with Proudhon knows that he was an anarchist, a foe of all government; yet few are able to

[18] "Résistance à la Révolution," reprinted in *I.G.*, p. 378.

[19] *I.G.*, pp. 173-74; *Justice*, II, 72.

[20] The typology of anti-hierarchic arguments used here is suggested by Sanford Lakoff's *Equality in Political Philosophy* (Cambridge, Mass., 1964). Lakoff tries to fit Proudhon into his scheme somewhere on the borderline between the liberals and the socialists but senses that he does not fit well into the slot assigned him. The reason is that Proudhon does not belong anywhere on the map Lakoff has charted. He is off by himself on some exotic island where the principle of distributive justice is not accepted.

account coherently for his objections. The reason why this aspect of his thought remains obscure is that it is part of a whole anarchist realm of discourse which is itself ill understood. Some remarks on the unfamiliar context of Proudhon's anarchism may help in its analysis.

One of the premises of anarchism is simply that because government is coercive and violent, it must be evil. Such a view is rather common. Luther, for instance, described political rule as "the fastening of wild and savage beasts with chains and bands . . . so that they must needs keep peace outwardly against their will" and found fault with it for doing so.[21] Rousseau returns to Luther's picture of government as an enchainer and also criticizes it on this ground. But neither Rousseau, nor Luther, nor most of the other writers who use this argument, qualify as anarchists. This position requires additional ingredients.

One reason Rousseau does not move from criticizing government to recommending its destruction is that he has a high regard for one of its essential features, lawmaking. "It is to the law alone that men owe justice and liberty," he declares.[22] Behind this statement lies the familiar argument that laws, being general and applicable only to external behavior, are self-limiting and hence praiseworthy. For Rousseau, these merits of legal control outweigh the disadvantages of political coercion. Government is indeed an enchainment, but if men are chained by laws, their bondage is salutary. For this reason Rousseau recommends not the destruction of government but its legal legitimization.

[21] Martin Luther, *Martin Luther: Selections from His Writings*, ed., John Dillenberger (New York, 1961), p. 370.
[22] Rousseau, p. 294, cf. Shklar, "Images," p. 922.

Rousseau's position suggests that another ingredient of full-blooded anarchism is antipathy toward law. Such antipathy takes many forms; the most prevalent involves reversing the usual argument in praise of law by criticizing its generality and externality. Luther makes both of these reversals. He finds fault with law's generality on the ground that this makes it too crude for dealing with the particular cases it is supposed to regulate. General rules cannot be adapted to the changing conditions they are meant to control. He concludes, "the body politic cannot be felicitously governed by rules."[23] This argument is really an objection to all rule-making, not only to legislation. Luther also attacks law's externality. By doing so he raises an objection to specifically legal rules. His point is that since law can only regulate overt conduct, it can do nothing to correct the thoughts and feelings that are the source of evil-doing.

Though Luther is critical of both law and government, he does not qualify as a full-blooded anarchist any more than does Rousseau. His ideal is certainly the absence of all legal and political regulation. "By the Spirit and by faith all Christians are throughout inclined to do well . . . much more than any one can teach them with all the laws and need so far as they are concerned no commandments nor law."[24] But he is unwilling to transform this vision into a proposal to abolish law and government, because, though he thinks that they are bad, he also regards them as indispensable. Most men are not Christians and so

[23] Luther, p. 331. This argument is ancient, going back to Plato, who, of course, used it for the perfection rather than the condemnation of government.

[24] *Ibid.*, p. 269.

cannot be freed from their coercive, crude, and external chains. If they were, being vicious, they would destroy each other.

Luther's insistence on the need for government suggests that still a third ingredient is required if anarchistic thinking is to count as unequivocal anarchism: the belief that government is unnecessary. This suggestion first appears in a developed form in the thought of William Godwin. So convinced was Godwin of society's aptitude for self-regulation that he thought law and government dispensable. His theory also contains anarchism's other two essentials: he condemns law as a procrustean bed, and government as unduly coercive.[25] By committing himself to all three of these positions, Godwin was able to take the step foreclosed to others: he could make a logically valid case for abolishing government and law.

This analysis shows what in Proudhon's critique of political rule bears most directly on his anarchism. The relevant points are his evaluation of government and law and his assessment of the need for them.

The starting point of his evaluation is Rousseauist, because he regards Rousseau's test for good government as compatible with the rules of respect. This test, as reformulated by Proudhon, is that "no one should obey a law unless he has consented to it himself."[26] For him as for Rousseau this belief leads immediately to a denunciation of every form of autocratic government. Since all autocra-

[25] D. H. Munro, *Godwin's Moral Philosophy* (Oxford, 1953), pp. 129, 151.
[26] *I.G.*, p. 267.

cies force their subjects to obey regulations they have not consented to, all must be condemned.

His premise also leads to denunciation of representative government. Like Rousseau, but in greater detail, Proudhon criticizes this kind of regime on the ground that representatives cannot express the will of their constituents. In a passage recalling Rousseau's remark that Englishmen are free only during parliamentary elections, he writes, "All citizens of the Second Republic are eligible ... to vote. . . . This moment of public political participation is short: forty-eight hours at the most for each election. . . . The President and the Representatives, once elected, are the masters: everything else obeys. It is subject, governable and taxable, without abatement."[27]

One reason why citizens are powerless between elections is that a deputy cannot work for all who vote for him, even if he knows what they want, because their objectives change and conflict.[28] The deputy also has environmentally produced motives for ignoring the aims of his electors. Anticipating numerous critics of the French parliament as a closed arena, Proudhon remarks that no sooner is a candidate elected than he acquires a new perspective on politics, as a member of the legislature, that gradually isolates him from his constituents.[29]

In Proudhon's eyes, it is as doubtful that representatives will respond to the desires of the public during elec-

[27] I.G., p. 226, cf. C.P., p. 283.
[28] Ibid., p. 210.
[29] "A propos de Louis Blanc," reprinted in I.G., p. 438; cf. Carnets, x, 52. Representative government is "a perpetual abuse of power for the profit of the reigning caste and the interests of representatives, against the interests of the represented."

tions as well as during the intervals between elections. The tragic results of numerous French elections had convinced him that voters often choose a candidate who does not even profess to support their views.[30] Since French voters have learned to choose more shrewdly since Proudhon's day, this argument no longer carries as much weight. But a final objection to representative government is as valid now as when Proudhon raised it. Electors cannot choose candidates responsive to their wishes because their political judgment is warped by membership in a hierarchic society. Being divided into inferiors and superiors, people vote "from motives of servility or hatred."[31] The mental blinders imposed by inequality keep them from understanding either the aims of the candidates or their own true interests.

Rousseau had not tested constitutional governments with his standard. Proudhon tries to fill the gap. It is true, he admits, that constitutional regimes are less oppressive than autocratic ones.[32] But their superiority is only marginal, because they are unstable. They are usually swept away by civil war if they do not degenerate into naked dictatorships.[33] Those that avoid these outcomes have an equally dismal end. They become secret instruments of bourgeois domination. The bourgeoisie thinks constitutionalism is better than autocracy for maintaining the

[30] *Sol.*, p. 48.    [31] *Conf.*, p. 229.
[32] *Conf.*, p. 221; but cf. *C.P.*, p. 377, where a constitution is called "a system at once wise, just and free." This enthusiasm is anomalous as Théodore Ruyssen shows in his introduction to *C.P.*, p. 123, but it also turns up in *Justice*, III, 277.
[33] *Conf.*, pp. 223, 230.

confidence so helpful in the quest for profit.[34] Hence, when it can do so, the bourgeoisie respects constitutional government's "legal forms, its juridical spirit, its reserved character, its parliamentary rituals."[35] Behind these trappings there lurks "a vast system of exploitation and intrigue, where politics is the counterpart of speculation, where taxation is but the payroll of a caste, and monopolized power the assistant to monopoly."[36]

Much of this critique sounds Marxian; but its theoretical basis is Proudhon's own. He calls constitutional government oppressive because it merely alleviates the symptoms of political illness while leaving their causes undisturbed. It accepts inequality as an unalterable fact, to be controlled, not removed. Then, in order to control inequality, government oppresses the upper strata to some degree, but the lower even more. By doing so government behaves disrespectfully, for in both cases it imposes regulations to which its subjects have not given their consent.[37]

Rousseau had criticized the representative, but not the democratic, aspect of representative democracy. Indeed, he had approved of the latter. Proudhon thinks he was mistaken in doing so. If an autocracy is unacceptable because it forces men to follow decisions that conflict with

[34] *Justice*, III, 145.    [35] *P.F.*, p. 304.
[36] *Ibid.*, cf. *Conf.*, p. 227.
[37] *P.F.*, pp. 245-47; *Conf.*, 217-18; *Carnets*, XI, p. 479: "Constitutional power is always arbitrary power, if not unstable power, lacking all character and morality. . . . To produce balance it is unnecessary to create a device that imposes it: it suffices to put [social] forces into the kind of agreement that induces them to hold one another in equilibrium."

their own, then direct democracy is also unacceptable since it too must sometimes prevent its subjects from executing their own decisions. In a direct democracy it is usually only the minority who are repressed, while in an autocracy the choices of everyone except the ruling elite are often blocked. But this difference in the amount of disrespect in the two regimes does not warrant a more favorable judgment of democracy; there is no reason to prefer the oppression of a majority to that of an autocrat.[38]

In at least one way, Proudhon finds democracy worse than dictatorship. The repression that an autocrat can impose is limited by the illegitimacy of his status. His subjects obey him from fear of disobedience, not because they accept his title to rule. The legitimacy of democratic regimes, on the other hand, is widely accepted, at least in modern times. Hence democratic governments can repress their subjects more outrageously than can autocracies.[39]

This argument no doubt goes too far. Though the range of alternatives open to democratic rulers may be wider than that available to autocrats, this does not mean democratic rulers can do anything they please. There are repressive policies they cannot follow, like massacring the innocent, which autocrats sometimes carry out with impunity. But whatever the weakness of Proudhon's argument, it does point to democracy's unprecedented capacity to mobilize and reshape society, a capacity that has had fateful consequences in our own time.

The most obvious objection to Proudhon's entire critique

[38] *I.G.*, pp. 208-16; *Cont.*, I, 340.
[39] *Sol.*, p. 48.

of existing government challenges its excessively formal view of the political process. It can be argued that just as too formal an analysis of British government was responsible for the mistaken thesis that Parliament is all-powerful, so Proudhon's failure to consider extra-legal influence in assessing the power of rulers leads him to underestimate their responsiveness to the wishes of the ruled.

The substance of this objection is undoubtedly correct. Proudhon takes no account of the informal pressures that even the most abject subjects exert on an autocrat. Nor does he consider the far more obvious influence of an electorate on its representatives. If he had done so, he could never have said that once in office deputies are exempt from all popular control.

But though the substance of the objection is correct—and it does reveal a shortcoming in Proudhon as a political analyst—it does not diminish his stature as a critic. His standard for judging governments would have required their condemnation even if he had been fully aware of the informal popular influence at work in them, because this influence only mitigates, and does not eliminate, disrespectful political coercion. Not even the most responsive government can dispense entirely with authority, "the right to command," no matter how elaborately it conceals this fact.[40] It is authority in this sense that Proudhon cannot abide. Thus the basis of his dislike for government is not a faulty analysis of the political process, but an exceedingly rigorous standard for judging it. As

---

[40] *Justice*, II, 312; cf. *Corr.*, IV, 149: "Organization of any kind is equivalent to the suppression of liberty, so far as free persons are concerned."

he said in 1848, explaining his vote against one of France's most democratic constitutions, "I voted against the Constitution, because it is a Constitution."[41] Any government, *ipso facto*, must be condemned.

In the final stage of his political critique, Proudhon turns the tables on Rousseau, by applying their common test of good government to his predecessor's scheme for an ideal one. Rousseau had sought a plan for political rule that would allow each citizen to execute his own decision whenever he obeyed the law. Had he found such a plan, Proudhon would surely have praised it, since it would have assured freedom of action. But he saw that Rousseau's attempt to design a respectful government was a failure and that his only accomplishment was to hide repression behind a libertarian mask. Hence he repeatedly criticizes Rousseau's ideal as "a theory destructive to liberty."[42]

The heart of Proudhon's objection to Rousseau is a denial of his claim that no coercion is inflicted by a properly constituted government when it forces a man to obey the law. Rousseau could say this because he used unusual conceptions of will and freedom. He thought of the will as having two parts, a particular or self-regarding part, and a part that is general or community-regarding. Freedom he conceived as the capacity for self-legislation, the ability to make and obey self-imposed laws. By distinguishing between self- and community-regarding will, and by conceiving of freedom as self-legislation, Rousseau laid a foundation for the view that liberty entails repres-

[41] *Conf.*, p. 215.    [42] *I.G.*, p. 193.

sion of will. If a man follows his self-regarding will when it conflicts with his community-regarding one, his action is not free. For when a self- and community-regarding will conflict, the action dictated by the self-regarding one cannot be made into a universally practicable action, i.e., a law. Consequently, if a man in such a situation is prevented by his government from following his self-regarding will, he is not constrained; rather, his opportunity to act freely is protected, for he retains the chance to follow his general will. Thus Rousseau's concept of the will as divided, and of liberty as self-legislation, serves as the theoretical basis for justifying coercion in the name of freedom.

Proudhon saw through this impressive bit of sophistry. The whole argument was nothing but an "enormous swindle,"[43] because a person kept from executing a selfish choice is in fact no less coerced than a person kept from executing a universalizable one. In neither case does government respect its subject's freedom of action, for in both it keeps him from doing what he wants to do.[44] Hence Rousseau's scheme of government does not succeed in eliminating disrespectful coercion. Rulers in his ideal state, as in any other, thwart achievement of their subjects' aims.

Why does Rousseau employ such peculiar and dangerous conceptions of will and freedom? Part of the explanation is his esteem for law. Since he regards legislation as highly desirable, he must deny it is coercive, for if obedience to law involves coercion, it cannot be desirable. His conceptions of freedom and will enable him

[43] *Justice*, III, 270.   [44] *Ibid.*, II, 362; *P.F.*, 345.

to do this. If obedience to universally applicable decisions does not curtail my freedom of action, then neither does legal compulsion to obey them. Similarly, if my liberty to do as I please is not reduced when I am kept from executing selfish decisions, then a legal ban on executing them does not curb it either. Rousseau's definitions serve to protect his defense of law's value from the charge that legislation can be oppressive.

As an anarchist, Proudhon finds fault not only with the coercion justified by Rousseau's political ideal, but also with the basis of that justification: Rousseau's esteem for law. It is true that Proudhon frequently opposed law as a mere symptom of more basic malaise, rather than as something inherently inadmissible.[45] Implicit in this way of arguing is the thesis that if society and government were not defective in the ways already analyzed, law would not be objectionable either.

But Proudhon also has some basic criticisms of legislation. Law puts "external authority . . . in the place of citizens' immanent, inalienable, untransferable authority."[46] There are two things wrong with law's externality. First, its method of enforcement, coercion by identifiable external agents, violates the second rule of respect by preventing the execution of decisions. The need for coercive enforcement makes law just as authoritarian, in Proudhon's eyes, as more arbitrary means of political control. The object to which law applies contributes further to its immorality. Law applies to overt behavior, not inward thought. It ignores, or at most gives minor attention to

[45] *I.G.*, p. 204.
[46] "Résistance à la Révolution," reprinted in *I.G.*, pp. 374, 378.

choices and aims, being content for the most part to consider action's form and results. The first rule of respect, on the other hand, calls for accepting the internal preliminaries to action, the decisions and purposes that direct it. From the standpoint of respect, law is thus blind to the kind of motivation worthy of the highest consideration.

Proudhon objects to more than the immediately disrespectful features of law's externality. He also denounces the externally oriented frame of mind encouraged by legal institutions. A society where the rule of law is dominant nurtures the sort of personality which "is convinced that the more or less improper acts that it performs every day, from morning to night, are necessary and hence legitimate, and that there is consequently no such thing as swindling or theft, except in the cases defined by law."[47] What is described here is the legalistic point of view personified by Shylock, which equates virtue with a legal claim and the just man with the lawful one. It sanctions judging others by how law-abiding they are, rather than by the degree to which they follow inwardly affirmed moral principles. Such an attitude is totally at odds with Proudhonian morality, since the rules of respect are precisely the sorts of moral principles it repudiates.

Though Proudhon fiercely attacks law's externality, he does not criticize its other trait: its generality. This is not surprising, since his whole ethical theory assumes that morality is a matter of accepting and following general rules. So strongly does Proudhon favor a rule-keeping morality that he thinks "the true judge for every man is

[47] *Cap.*, p. 227; cf. *Cont.*, ii, 219-20.

his own conscience, a fact that implies replacement of the system of courts and laws with a system of personal obligations and contracts, in other words, suppression of legal institutions."[48] On the surface, this statement may seem totally hostile to law. But it is also partial to a legalistic conception of morality that pictures conscience as a judge who decides which of several rules governing conduct and choice applies to a particular case. Having approved of general principles in the moral realm, Proudhon could hardly object to law on the ground that it used them. He quarreled with law only because it was external, not because it was general. General *moral* rules, being applicable to choice, are praiseworthy.

But though Proudhon does not condemn the generality of legal regulation, he does consider it. His point is that law cannot be general enough to avoid being arbitrary. "Laws in small number! . . . Why, that is impossible. Mustn't the government regulate all interests and judge all claims? Well, owing to the nature of society, interests are innumerable, their relations are variable and infinitely changeable: how can it possibly make few laws? How can they be simple?"[49] A complicated code of detailed laws, the only kind that can be effective, "sows disorder in men's minds, obscures the notion of justice . . . and makes necessary a whole caste of interpreters to explain the system."[50] Laws must be so numerous, complicated, specific, changeable, so subject to twisted interpretation, so incomprehensible, that they must oppress. Only a rule that is "unchanging," "supremely intelligible," "the inviolable standard of all human actions," in short, as general as

[48] *Conf.*, p. 236.    [49] *I.G.*, p. 205.    [50] *Cont.*, I, 337.

possible, is sanctioned by the ethics of respect.[51] Since law cannot have these attributes, it must be fundamentally condemned.

Proudhon's critique of law helps to explain his opposition to Rousseau's ideal state. He not only objected to the coercion justified by Rousseau's ideal; he did not think the benefit gained by justifying it was worth the price. Rousseau may perhaps have realized that the man who is kept from following his self-regarding will is, in a sense, just as constrained as the one kept from following his general will. But since self-regarding wills cannot be universalized, the cost of repressing them could not strike him as high, while the benefit of doing so seemed enormous. If some people were now and then kept from following their worthless particular wills, all would benefit immensely. For then everyone would follow the law. To Proudhon, on the other hand, who fundamentally disapproved of law, the cost of such repression seemed enormous, and its benefits negligible.

The first two ingredients in Proudhon's anarchism—his objections to government and law—ally to support a sweeping denunciation of rulership. His hostility toward political coercion prompts him to apply Rousseau's test of good government just as rigorously as its inventor had done. His opposition to law leads him to extend its application to areas from which Rousseau had excluded it and to detect coercion where Rousseau, with his admiration for law, had professed to see freedom. But all this criticism of government and legislation, however vigorous, would not support their abolition, unless Prou-

[51] *Justice*, I, 426.

dhon's theory contained anarchism's third essential: the belief that political rule is unnecessary.

Proudhon does indeed hold this belief, but in a rather sophisticated form, easier to defend than the dogmatic assertions that government is needless, made by anarchists like Tolstoy. The statements of Tolstoy, and writers like him, give whatever backing there is to anarchism's reputation as a naïve belief in government's easy dispensability.[52] Proudhon, of course, is more circumspect. His theory of political development kept him from thinking government easily dispensable, because it asserted that until his own time government had performed vital functions by building character, extirpating laziness, and so on. Even in his own day, its abolition could not seem easy to Proudhon; his reflections on human nature and society had convinced him that government continued to perform the valuable service of maintaining order and that, if it were abolished, some substitute would have to be found.

The question of the need for political rule thus depended on whether government was indispensable for the maintenance of order. Proudhon denied that it was. To begin with, government was certainly not a logical requisite for order, though as the expression "law and order" shows, the two are often equated in common usage. "*Order* is a genus, *government*, a species. In other words, there are several ways to conceive of order: what proof is there that order in society is of the sort its masters wish to assign to it?"[53] Nor could government be considered a

[52] Isaiah Berlin, "Tolstoy and Enlightenment," *Encounter*, xvi, No. 2 (February 1961), p. 38.
[53] *I.G.*, p. 202.

causal requisite for order. Causal *necessity* does not exist, at least in human affairs, where innovation can occur.[54] As for the causal *connection* between government and order, it was proved tenuous by the not infrequent failure of political rule to control conflict.[55] Thus the need for government in civilized societies was extremely dubious, though ironclad proof of its dispensability depended on discovery of a suitable replacement. When this conclusion was added to Proudhon's denunciation of government, unmitigated anarchism resulted. Government was in most respects profoundly evil. Its one good effect could be achieved by some other means; hence it ought to be eliminated.

To many realists arrival at such a judgment would be a signal for re-examining first principles. Something must be wrong with values and analysis which imply that indispensable institutions like government and law, not to mention hierarchy, must be abolished. To other realists, these conclusions would suggest not revision, but withdrawal. Denunciation of the actual would not be diluted, but attempts to improve it would be abandoned. To Proudhon, however, as a true radical, these findings occasion no such second thoughts. Instead, they give impetus to further theorizing. Having proved to his satisfaction that hierarchy and political authority should be abolished, he presses on to discover new arrangements that will vindicate his case by making superior substitutes available. The obverse of his radical critique is a proposal for fundamental change.

[54] *Justice*, III, 173.  [55] *I.G.*, p. 302.

# CHAPTER V

## Proudhon as a Rebuilder of Society

THE prescriptive side of Proudhon's theory is the part most crucial for its overall validity. Both his criticism of existing institutions and his contention that history has reached the point where institutions can be abolished rest on the claim that superior substitutes can be established. If this claim should prove unfounded, the critical and historical parts of his theory would be called into question.

To count as superior from Proudhon's point of view, replacements for existing institutions must pass two tests. They must do the job of conflict management now carried out by government and hierarchy. In addition, they must permit men who accept and try to follow the rules of respect to succeed in doing so. Proudhon's reformative endeavor is a determined search for substitutes having these qualifications. He tries to describe arrangements that neither jeopardize social order nor stand in the way of his ideals.

### The Dangers of Anarchy: Hobbes and Proudhon

Since Proudhon regarded hierarchy and government as the wellsprings of degradation, he might have said that any environment in which they are lacking is both safe and respectful. Yet he did not. While insisting that these impediments to freedom and justice were incompatible with respect, he also saw that their absence was an insufficient condition for its attainment. The source of this insight is Proudhon's conviction that in a society without government and hierarchy a Hobbesian state of nature must arise, for under such conditions "our irascible appetite pushes us toward war."[1] A world free of contemporary society's two great plagues would not be respectful, because then the order-maintaining function would be unfulfilled.

Although Proudhon accepts Hobbes' description of the state of nature, he criticizes Hobbes' explanation of it. This criticism enables him to reject Hobbes' remedy. Hobbes ascribes natural war to aggressive desires so powerful that they can be neither eradicated nor weakened. Since these desires are uncontrollable, the only way to prevent their translation into hostile acts is by legal deterrence. Men must be frightened into behaving peacefully by threats of punishment from an absolute government. The trouble with this argument, according to Proudhon, is that it rests on "the most unfavorable hypothesis" about the cause of conflict.[2] The truth is that even in the state of nature conflict springs not primarily from aggressive desires, but from competition for scarce goods and for attainment of incompatible ideals. War is far more a clash of interests and principles than of domineering passions.[3] It is true that the only way to prevent the conflict that is motivated by a desire to dominate is with legal deterrence, but since antagonism springs mostly from pursuit of interests and ideals, a more respectful remedy can be found, at least in principle.

[1] *G.P.*, p. 121.     [2] *Ibid.*, p. 118.     [3] *Ibid.*, pp. 55, 93.

Proudhon's attitude toward Hobbes complicates his reformative endeavor by making it hard to describe respectful institutions that are also safe. On the one hand, the description of respectful arrangements is complicated by misgivings about their safety. Proudhon fears that any institutions that could count as respectful would allow so much antagonism that Hobbes' nightmarish state of nature would become a reality. On the other hand, the description of safe institutions is plagued by doubts about respectfulness. If Proudhon is careful to describe safe arrangements, he may end with institutions that are even less respectful than existing ones. Fearing Hobbes' nightmare, he is in constant danger of accepting its describer's antidote.

## *The Illusions of Laissez-Faire*

At the time Proudhon was writing, an inviting way out of this dilemma was being vigorously urged by the economic liberals. In their opinion, conflict could be respectfully managed, provided that it occurred within the framework of free markets. There the price system gives cues to each trader that prompt him to act so as to satisfy others as he satisfies himself. If a buyer sets a low price, in order to get the better of a seller, the seller finds another customer who respects the terms of trade set by the market. Conversely, if a seller tries to exploit a buyer by demanding a price above that fixed by the market, his customer turns to another supplier who adheres to the established price. Hence in the market, as described by its defenders, no man's conduct or choice is constrained by another, yet any action that occurs benefits all men.

Proudhon was strongly attracted by this doctrine, because it promised exactly the kind of regulation he was seeking. "The disciples of Malthus and Say, vigorously rejecting state intervention in commercial and industrial affairs, take every opportunity to glory in their liberal appearance and pretend that they are more revolutionary than the revolution."[4] But Proudhon saw through the liberating promise of laissez-faire. He was sure that the price mechanism was just as oppressive as law and government. Because "more than one honest soul had been taken in" by the wiles of the economists, Proudhon painstakingly refuted them.[5] It was important for him to do so, since their position was so similar to his that the two risked being confused.

To begin with, Proudhon points out that actual market prices vary widely and unpredictably, sometimes to the benefit of buyers, sometimes to that of sellers. Economic transactions cued by the price mechanism are a kind of lottery, over whose outcome traders have no control.[6] At one time or another swings in price may grant each trader a windfall. What is certain is that they cause widespread interference with goal attainment, by depriving many persons of a secure income.

If all had an equal chance to benefit from the risk built into the price mechanism, it might still be admissible as a method for organizing society. But in fact the law of supply and demand is a "deceitful law . . . suitable only for assuring the victory of the strong over the weak, of those who own property over those who own nothing."[7] It is

[4] *I.G.*, p. 284.   [5] *Ibid.*   [6] *Justice*, II, 147.
[7] *Cap.*, p. 141.

not true that all traders are equally subject to the market. In many cases a few have sufficient control of resources to influence or even determine price. In those cases all the others must choose between submitting to the monopolist's terms or foregoing any purchase of the commodity he offers. When that commodity is employment, even this choice is lacking. Hence the market does not fulfill its promise of protection for each man's freedom to pursue his goals.

Economists could contest the preceding argument by pointing to its misconstruction of their viewpoint. They contend only that free markets protect freedom, not that monopolists do. To back up this thesis, the economists ascribe the same inevitability to the laws of the free market that is a feature of natural scientific laws. No one is coerced by another when he refrains from building below the high-water mark. Since economic laws are just as inevitable as those of nature, no one is coerced by another when he refrains from selling above the market price. To this argument Proudhon replies that whatever may be the proper attitude toward natural necessity, acceptance of market prices as inevitable, and hence coercionless, is in error. The market is manmade; hence any constraint it imposes is the coercion of man by man.[8]

Proudhon's final, simplest, and most devastating point is that free enterprise, being "unable to solve its celebrated problem of the harmony of interests, [is forced] to impose laws, if only provisional ones, and abdicates in its turn before this new authority that is incompatible with the practice of liberty."[9] In the end, laissez-faire has to rely

[8] *Justice*, ii, 92-93, 147-48.　　[9] *Ibid.*, i, 305.

on political coercion, if only in the person of a night watchman, to assure the safety of its scheme. Thus the market, called into question by its own shortcomings, is definitively refuted by its resort to the very coercion it promises to avoid.

Although Proudhon repudiates most aspects of laissez-faire, he does find a use for one of its features: competition. The market and the price system are oppressive fakes, but competition is "the spice of exchange, the salt of work. To suppress competition is to suppress liberty itself; it is to begin the restoration of the old regime from below, by putting work back under the system of favoritism and abuse from which '89 has emancipated it."[10] This text makes clear that Proudhon is no ordinary socialist critic of free enterprise, eager to drown competitive relations in a sea of cooperation. Nor is he as fearful as are writers like Hobbes of the conflict that such relations allow. Rather than wanting to do away with the rivalries celebrated by the economists, Proudhon seeks to preserve and perfect them, for he sees in them an enormous creative potential. Within the framework of the market, competition, "lacking a higher regulative principle, has been perverted."[11] It becomes an instrument for imposing exploitative prices on helpless victims. But in a more appropriate environment, it could have salutary effects. Though "com-

[10] *I.G.*, p. 132; cf. *Cont.*, I, 212. At least one eminent critic has been so impressed with Proudhon's attack on free enterprise that he overlooked his defense of competition. According to Isaiah Berlin, "Competition . . . was to Proudhon the greatest of evils," *Karl Marx* (2d ed., London, 1948), p. 113.

[11] *I.G.*, p. 132.

petition today" is "the cause of the weak's oppression," in tomorrow's respectful society it may become "his strength and his guarantee."[12]

## The Virtues of Bargaining

The crux of Proudhon's respectful society is the bargaining process. His ideal world is one in which individuals and groups bargain directly with each other for all the things they want, without any intermediaries, until they arrive at mutually acceptable terms of agreement. The great virtue of this practice is its compatibility with man's freedom to do as he pleases. According to Proudhon, a bargainer, unlike a trader on a market, a holder of a rank, or a subject of a state, need not submit to restraints upon his action. He can arrange to do exactly as he pleases, by working out terms of agreement acceptable to others. The bargaining relationship "imposes no obligation on its parties but that which results from their personal promise; . . . it is subject to no external authority. . . . When I bargain for some good with one or more of my fellow citizens, it is clear that then it is my will alone that is my law."[13] If this is true, then bargaining, unlike all other patterns of social relations, accords with the rule of respect enjoining freedom of action.

Although Proudhon does not explicitly test bargaining with the rule of respect that prescribes identification with the purposes of others, it clearly accords with that norm. If I am to come to terms with another, I must identify with his purposes so as to make concessions that will be

[12] *Mel.*, ii, 2.
[13] *I.G.*, pp. 188, 267.

attractive to him. The bargaining process encourages precisely the sort of reciprocal acceptance of purposes that is required by Proudhon's highest value.

So much for bargaining's respectful promise. It can be likened to Hope, which remained in Pandora's box after she had let out all the malicious forces that plague mankind. For advocacy of bargaining as the only pattern of social relations raised serious difficulties, and its advantages remained a distant prospect. Proudhon had to find some way to push the difficulties back into Pandora's box, while coaxing the promise out into practicality.

Insecurity is the most obvious danger faced by a society where bargaining is the only interactional pattern. In such a society, bargaining relationships are likely to degenerate into struggles and, ultimately, into dictated settlements. When a party is in a position to impose terms on others, rather than to make concessions, there will be nothing to keep him from doing so. In short, members of a society of bargainers run a grave risk of being crushed by their rivals.[14]

Another problem faced by bargainers is disrespectful thought and action. This problem may be less dangerous, but to Proudhon it is just as serious. Bargaining aims at

[14] This analysis of bargaining was suggested by Martin Meyerson and Edward Banfield, *Politics, Planning and the Public Interest* (Glencoe, 1955), pp. 306-307. Other helpful discussions of bargaining are Neil Chamberlain, *A General Theory of Economic Process* (New York, 1955), pp. 74-160; Carl J. Friedrich, *Man and His Government* (New York, 1963), pp. 484-501; Robert A. Dahl and Charles E. Lindblom, *Politics, Economics and Welfare* (New York, 1953), pp. 324-33, 472-93; Brian Barry, *Political Argument* (London, 1965), pp. 84-91.

compromise, at agreement involving mutual concessions on a quid pro quo basis. Settlements of this sort have always offended rule-minded moralists, and Proudhon is no exception. The trouble with agreement by reciprocal concession is that considerations of moral principle are left out.[15] A bargainer tries to reach the most satisfactory terms he can. These terms may turn out to be morally valid, but they are not arrived at by applying some ethical standard deemed relevant to the contested issue. The only relevant consideration is the relative power of the opposed parties. To Proudhon, this is inadmissible. The rules of respect must be obeyed even when they are unprofitable. Yet a bargainer in a favorable power position will disregard respect's imperatives if he can make a better deal by doing so. An intolerable gap thus separates Proudhon's principles from the practice that is supposed to reflect them.

## Mutualist Society

In order to protect bargainers from being crushed by their rivals, Proudhon seeks to equalize their power. He thinks combat and dictation can be avoided by arranging society so that its "component groups remain equal," for then "none wins preponderance over the others."[16]

The reason some contenders are more powerful than others, according to Proudhon, is that "heterogeneous forces" are "permanently amalgamated and fused" within them."[17] Hence an end to unequal bargaining power calls for distributing these heterogeneous forces more evenly

[15] Meyerson and Banfield, p. 309.
[16] *Justice*, ii, 262.       [17] *G.P.*, p. 133.

among contenders, so that each of them is reciprocally but not essentially dependent on the others. It is hard to know exactly what Proudhon has in mind when he calls for an even distribution of heterogeneous forces, because he does not say what these forces represent. He may mean the capacity to control the supply of goods sought by others. A party who controls the supply of many goods sought by others has greater bargaining power than they. If this interpretation is acceptable, then what Proudhon intends by calling for an even distribution of heterogeneous forces is that every contender must control the supply of some goods that others seek and must not depend entirely on any other for satisfaction of his own wants.

Proudhon is vague about the structure of a society organized according to this principle. Perhaps the example of the utopians had taught him that it is tactically unwise to draw blueprints, because they divert attention from immediate action to an uncertain future. At any rate, almost all that can be said about the structure of his ideal, "mutualist" society is that it consists of numerous bargaining units, some of which offer the same good, and none of which supply too many goods.[18] Concerning one

[18] Proudhon did not favor a society composed of small groups, as Martin Buber contends. Buber regards Proudhon as an advocate of face-to-face contacts for their own sake and claims him as a partisan of "the local community or commune, living on the strength of its own interior relationships," *Paths in Utopia* (Boston, 1958), p. 28. It is true that occasional notes of this sort creep into some of Proudhon's last writings, but they are absent from his most systematic works. In these, the point of social reconstruction is not to vitalize the primary community but to organize a large society in a respectful way. For this purpose, a reduction in group

detail of social organization he is more explicit. He stresses the need to strengthen the workers' bargaining position. This recommendation is the main point of one of his more obscure doctrines: his theory of collective force.

Unless this doctrine is seen as part of Proudhon's theory of bargaining, it is rather puzzling. He first mentioned it in an account, in *Propriété*, of the erection of the Luxor obelisque. Collective force is described as "that immense force which results from workers' union and harmony, from the convergence and simultaneousness of their efforts. . . . Two hundred grenadiers placed the Luxor obelisque on its base in a few hours; do you really think a single man could have succeeded in two hundred days?"[19] Having made this claim for the workers, Proudhon could be expected to urge a higher remuneration for their labor; but he does not. The argument, both in *Propriété* and elsewhere, is left hanging; it contributes to Proudhon's critique of existing conditions and even helps explain it, but does not directly support any of his proposals for change.

---

size may sometimes be useful: when it helps equalize bargaining power. Other circumstances may call for an increase in dimension. In fact, Proudhon is quite willing to favor large organizations, if they will increase the control of weak contenders over the goods they supply. Large groups can help support the bargaining process provided they do not become so large as to unilaterally control the supply of important goods. *I.G.*, p. 270; *Cap.*, pp. 190-91; *Carnets*, III, 114. It is also noteworthy that Proudhon, besides defending large groups, also denounced the petty surveillance prevalent in the small communities which Buber thinks he favors. "If authority is painful, the jealousy of confreres is no easier to put up with," *Carnets*, VI, 88.

[19] *Prop.*, p. 215.

Seen in the context of his theory of bargaining, however, the doctrine of collective force becomes more com-
prehensible; it appears as an argument for strengthening
the workers' bargaining position in order to protect them
from exploitation. By calling attention to their collective
force, Proudhon hopes to increase their power and make
them less dependent on their employers.[20]

If peaceful bargaining is to be assured, something more
is needed than equalization of the contenders' power.
Combat might break out between the units of the egalitarian society envisaged by Proudhon. For one thing, the
balancing of power relations would encourage deadlock.
This in turn might easily lead to aggression. Contenders
who are reciprocally but not essentially dependent on one
another will probably begin working for their ends by
making concessions. The cost of dictating terms is too
high, because parties can always turn to other suppliers
or do without the good offered. For the same reason, the
rejection of all proposed compromise settlements will be
easy. If I can turn to other suppliers of the good one of
them offers me, or dispense with it altogether, my incentive to agreement with him will be small. Where power
relations among contenders are equal, few bargains will
be struck. In the limiting case, no social interaction may
occur at all. But if this outcome seemed imminent, the relative cost of combat would decline. The need for con-
certed action would come to outweigh the high cost of
attempting to organize it by force.

Some such anticipation is at the root of Proudhon's fear
that if "the same kind of power is distributed among dif-

[20] *G.P.*, p. 132.

ferent persons, . . . [they] are neutralized by competition and anarchy."[21] At most, "a weak, more or less precarious society will emerge."[22] A society whose units are too autonomous is just as unstable as one where they are hierarchically organized. The line between pluralism and fragmentation is extremely thin. "Imagine a society where all relations between individuals had just ceased, where each one provided for his living in absolute isolation. . . . Just like a piece of matter whose molecules had lost the rapport that makes them cohere, it would crumble into dust at the slightest shock."[23]

To ward off this fate, Proudhon relies on social diversity. Along with "the greatest independence of individuals and groups" must go "the greatest possible variety of combinations."[24] Or, as he says in another place, it is not enough to create "independent centers"; numerous "specialties" are needed too.[25] The units of a mutualist society are not only to be equal in power; they are also to differ in their occupations, personalities, ideas, inclinations, and any other characteristics that may affect the quality of the goods they offer. Equality of rank must be supplemented by diversity of kind.

Social diversity deters bargaining stalemate by increasing the incentive of equally powerful contenders to compromise. I will be more eager to reach agreement with a supplier who offers me an unusual good, *ceteris paribus*, than with one who can provide only an ordinary one. By making available a wide variety of goods, social diversity

---

[21] *Ibid.*, pp. 133-34.  [22] *Justice*, IV, 263.  [23] *Ibid.*, II, 259.
[24] *Ibid.*, III, 429.  [25] *Cap.*, p. 189; cf. *Avert.*, p. 197.

gives an impetus to joint action without going so far as to encourage dictated settlements.[26]

Even if social diversity deterred the threat of strife raised by stalemate, it could not ward off another danger to the integrity of bargaining. Contenders who had strong incentives to compromise their differences might have even stronger motives for imposing terms. They would try to force their opponents to submit, in spite of all inducements to bargain. This would be the case for any contender who sought ideological rather than material advantages. A person who is out to win converts to his point of view cannot make concessions to his adversaries, even for profit. As Proudhon puts it, matters of principle "are not things over which one bargains."[27] To compromise here "would be like forgery by a public scribe, a crime for which conscience could find no excuse."[28] In other words, Proudhon's social arrangements seem to invite resort to combat for the settlement of ideological disputes.

This accusation is unfounded, because it overlooks the unanimous agreement about respect's intrinsic goodness, presupposed by his whole reformative venture. In his en-

---

[26] It is of course true that Proudhon's aims of equalizing the power of contenders and increasing their diversity are far from compatible. Under conditions of perfect social diversity each contender would be the unique supplier of some good and hence would have monopoly control. If the good were a vital one, his monopoly would give him a great power advantage over other parties. The problem of reconciling the two objectives is therefore great, but this does not necessarily vitiate their merit. The thesis that diversity can neutralize the disadvantages of equal power still deserves serious attention.

[27] G.P., p. 201.

[28] Justice, III, 275.

visioned society there may be "diversities of opinion," but "nothing that divides men . . . exists any longer among mutualist groups."[29] Ideological disputes simply cannot arise under mutualism. No matter how devoted a contender may be to an ideal, he will sacrifice it if he must do so to preserve the integrity of his universally accepted highest value.

Though principled disagreement does not endanger Proudhonian bargaining, other contingencies do: fraud and conspiracy. Even if mutualist social arrangements made combat and dictation unprofitable, they would leave the door open to these covert strategies for undermining the bargaining process. A person could misrepresent the value of the good he offered. He could ally himself with a few others in order to increase their joint bargaining power over the rest. He could conspire with another in order to reach mutually beneficial settlements that were injurious to a third party. If any one of these abuses became at all widespread, the balanced power relationships needed for safe bargaining would be destroyed.

Proudhon has little confidence in the integrity of bargainers. "Most of the time they are two swindlers who try to cheat each other reciprocally."[30] The threat of fraud and conspiracy is serious for him. It is one of the considerations which ultimately force him to admit that no social arrangements, however ideal, can by themselves safeguard peace.

Another consideration reinforces this conclusion. The equality of power in a mutualist society may facilitate bargaining between parties who want complementary goods,

[29] *Cap.*, p. 218.     [30] *Ibid.*, p. 137.

but it also encourages bitter rivalry among seekers of the same good, especially if the good is scarce. Unequally powerful contenders will seldom struggle for an advantage in short supply, such as a good job; the prize will usually go to the strongest without a fight. But if contenders enjoy equal bargaining power, they are likely to fight hard for the good they seek. "Between individuals of equal power and similar pretensions, there is naturally antagonism."[31] In spite of all precautions, it looks as if Hobbes' nightmare may still become a reality in a mutualist society. For Hobbes had long ago pointed out that "any two men" with equal power who "desire the same thing, which nevertheless they cannot both enjoy . . . become enemies; and in the way to their end . . . endeavor to destroy or subdue one another."[32]

The conclusion is obvious, and Proudhon draws it. Mutualist society, like any other, "cannot depend on the calculations and propriety of egoism." To think otherwise is to be duped by the myth of spontaneous harmony.[33] Must it also be admitted that mutualist society cannot dispense with the orthodox techniques for managing conflict—law, government and hierarchy?

[31] *Justice*, IV, 263.
[32] Thomas Hobbes, *Leviathan*, ed. A. D. Lindsay (New York, 1950), p. 102.
[33] *Justice*, I, 316; cf. III, 519. Proudhon sometimes took an easy and inadequate way around the problems faced by his scheme for structural reform, by resorting to the dictum that men would learn to bargain peacefully simply by living in a mutualist society. The member of a mutualist society, Proudhon sometimes contends, "is not the same. . . . His conscience is different, his self is changed," *Justice*, I, 420; cf. *ibid.*, II, 261; IV, 366.

## The Mutualist Norm: Commutative Justice

Proudhon of course denies this. He admits that mutualist society is an inadequate guarantee of a safe, respectful world. But he thinks consideration of its inadequacy shows how to improve it. The defect in mutualist organization is its one-sided way of managing conflict. It assumes that combat and bargaining are the sole forms of contention. If this were true, power alone would have to be controlled, since the outcome of combat and bargaining depends on the comparative strength of opposed parties. But, in fact, relative power is just one of the forces that affect the outcome of disputes. Equally influential are the views of contenders about the merits of their conflicting claims. Since disputes may be settled by discussion on merits as well as by bargaining on a quid pro quo basis, an adequate guarantee of a safe, respectful world must regulate both.

For this reason, Proudhon prescribes a standard of merit, "a rule for all bargains" to regulate contenders' claims of right, just as mutualist society regulates their assertions of power.[34] The standard he turns to is the rule of commutative justice, which imposes on each contender the duty to give goods to all others that are just as valuable as those he receives from them. It obliges equivalent exchange.

A case can be made that the rule of commutative justice is so formal and empty that it cannot possibly control opposed claims, as Proudhon hopes. Even if I follow the injunction to give the equivalent of what I receive, in any

[34] *I.G.*, p. 206; cf. *Justice*, 1, 304.

particular exchange I can justify giving whatever amount of good I please, since the commutative rule says nothing about how the value of what I have received, or its equivalent, should be determined. If, for example, I think the eminence of its owner determines the value of a good, the commutative norm supports my giving a fabulous sum for a lock of Lord Byron's hair. If, on the other hand, the cost of production of a good is my evaluative standard, the same norm authoritizes me to give an infinitesimal payment for it. It follows that since the number of possible evaluative criteria is infinite, so are the duties that commutative justice may impose.

This argument goes too far.[35] It is no doubt true that the obligation to exchange equivalently enjoins no particular actions. But it is not devoid of all specific meaning because it *excludes* certain sorts of conduct, such as the uncompensated acquisition of goods, i.e., theft. To oblige people to give the equivalent of what they receive is at least to prohibit them from taking goods without some kind of payment. This prohibition is important, because it bans the most oppressive type of dictated settlement: that which denies a contender any compensation at all for the good he supplies.

Another kind of action prohibited by the commutative rule is fraud. Commutative justice binds contenders to make sincere appraisals of the goods they offer, and to measure the comparative worth of goods offered to them

---

[35] My defense of commutative justice owes much to Judith Shklar's remarks in *Legalism* (Cambridge, Mass., 1964), pp. 113-23.

with the same standard. People may not deliberately deceive one another.[36]

But commutative justice is most conducive to peaceful contention in giving parties a common standard for testing the merits of their respective claims. Having this standard in common makes them less likely to fight, because it gives them an opportunity to discuss the merits of their differences, when the possibilities of bargaining have been exhausted. Hence the prospects for mutualism would brighten considerably if all contenders followed the commutative rule. A climate of opinion would arise to give much needed support to the social process relied on by Proudhon to realize his ideals.

## The Productivity Standard and the Failure of Mutualism

Nevertheless, commutative justice is an inadequate regulative principle for mutualist society. Because it sets no single criterion for measuring value, it allows each contender to use whatever standard he prefers, provided that he uses it fairly. This permissiveness is dangerous. Differences will not be resolved, even between parties who accept the commutative rule, whenever they choose different appraising standards. For then, though they both contend in good faith, the settlement that seems fair to one will necessarily seem unfair to the other. The commutative rule is for this reason a "fine maxim, but a vague one," which cannot assure the viability of mutualism.[37]

In his zeal to remove the vagueness from commutative justice, Proudhon makes the prescriptive part of his

[36] *I.G.*, pp. 287-89.  [37] *Prog.*, p. 82.

theory inconsistent, by building into mutualism something incompatible with the rules of respect. What he says is that contenders must use the same standard for measuring the value of goods, their cost of production. "Every product will be paid for with a product that costs the same sum of labor and expense."[38] The trouble with this principle is that it implants in Proudhon's ideal society precisely the sort of distributive standard that he condemns in existing society. If "income must be equivalent to productivity," then contenders who offer goods that cost a lot to produce deserve higher rewards than those who offer cheaply created ones.[39] As Proudhon himself admitted, "The superior worker, who understands and executes faster than another, and who turns out more products of better quality, will receive a larger reward, because he surpasses the common measure With all the more reason, so will the worker who combines management skill and leadership talent with manual ability. He will be able to earn the equivalent of one and a half, two, three or even more standard daily wages."[40]

The same points that Proudhon makes against inequality of rank in general obviously apply to the kind of hierarchy he defends here. He has recommended a distributive principle—to each according to his productive contribution—that on his own reasoning must entail degrading distinctions. The rich, in a mutualist society as in any other, will more readily win acceptance for their aims than the poor, and will be favored in their attempts to reach them.

[38] *Cap.*, p. 146.     [39] *Prog.*, p. 82.
[40] *Cap.*, p. 150; cf. *Justice*, III, 128.

This inconsistency in Proudhon's theory is often overlooked. Léon Walras, for example, far from detecting hierarchic implications in Proudhon's views on the distribution of wealth, described it as that of "all the egalitarians: men are absolutely and naturally equal. Hence social wealth should be distributed equally among them."[41]

One reason why Walras and others miss the inegalitarianism implicit in Proudhon's distributive criterion is that it is very well hidden. It is obscured by the thesis that the productivity standard calls for use of the same *units*, but not the same *method* of measuring value. Were this the case, it would be true that the productivity standard entailed no inequality, since use of common units of measurement, such as the dollar system, does not cause inequality.[42] But the productivity standard does fix a method for determining value. It is analogous to the canons by which measurements of price are made, rather than to the units such as dollars in which they are expressed.

The hierarchic implications of the productivity standard are also hidden behind predictions of imminent equality. While admitting that his standard licenses inequality, Proudhon sometimes predicts that its use will put an end to disparities of wealth. "The theory of human justice, in which reciprocity of respect is converted into reciprocity of service, leads closer and closer to equality in all things." "In less than two generations, all vestiges of inequality

---

[41] Léon Walras, *L'économie politique et la justice* (Paris, 1860), p. 44. But Walras did have doubts about the consistency of Proudhon's egalitarianism, cf. pp. 48, 50, 52.

[42] *Cap.*, p. 202.

will have disappeared."[43] Yet nowhere is a case made for
this assertion. It is nothing but a hope for the future used
to cover up a moral incongruity.

That Proudhon fell back on a distributive principle is
especially disappointing because his work sometimes hints
at a promising alternative. Had he pursued it, he might
have transformed commutative justice into an effective
safeguard for mutualism. He sometimes suggests that a
person contemplating a transaction be left free to choose
his own standard of appraisal, provided that his choice is
acceptable to the others. Put another way, criteria of evaluation should be as subject to compromise and discussion as
other terms of exchange. Then appraisal would be made
according to a wide variety of standards, "in some cases
according to the quality of workmanship, in others according to intelligence, in still others according to payment given or promised, etc."[44] Adherence to this procedure would prevent the stalemate and warfare that are
the likely outcomes of contention regulated by the vague
commutative norm. This procedure would therefore reach
the same end as the productivity standard, but it would
also surpass that standard by averting inequality of wealth.
If evaluative criteria were objects of contention, no one
standard for distributing reward would be used. Hence
the same persons could not always get the highest com-
pensations. Instead, each would receive different appraisals and payments for the goods he offered from different
contenders, and different appraisals and payments from

[43] *Justice*, ii, 75; iii, 96; cf. *Cont.*, ii, 289.
[44] *G.P.*, p. 129.

the same contender at different times. As a result of having the goods he offered subject to constantly changing evaluations, no person would have a fixed economic status. For society as a whole the result would be exactly that sought by mutualist structural principles: "equivalence amidst diversity."[45] Hence, if Proudhon had developed his hints about making standards of evaluation objects of contention, he might have devised a mutualist principle that conformed to respect's imperatives.

The fact remains that he did not pursue this alternative very far and that the way he used for closing the loophole in commutative justice entails thought and behavior forbidden by his ultimate value. The most that can be said in defense of the productivity standard is that it is somewhat less disrespectful than likely alternatives. One of Proudhon's reasons for thinking this is shaky. According to him it is a fact that under mutualism "wealth becomes the general condition."[46] If this were true, inequality

[45] *Cont.*, II, 189. In his remarks on "Super-Subordination without Degradation," Georg Simmel develops Proudhon's hints in a way similar to mine, but Simmel relies hardly at all on Proudhon's writings for his interpretation. See *The Sociology of Georg Simmel*, ed. Kurt H. Wolff (Glencoe, 1950), p. 285.

[46] *Justice*, II, 6. Some writers claim that Proudhon's prediction of abundance is not only unfounded, but also contradicted by other parts of his theory, e.g., Henri Bachelin, *P.-J. Proudhon, socialiste nationale* (Paris, 1941), p. 151. To them, Proudhon is an ascetic who both disliked abundance and thought it unattainable. The first of these claims arises from confusing Proudhon's opposition to great inequality of wealth with antipathy to prosperity as such. Actually, Proudhon was not hostile to affluence. In fact, he favored it, provided it was fairly shared. His main economic objective was to "have as much as possible produced and consumed,

would begin above such a high floor that it would not produce attitudes and conduct as disrespectful as those that occur where disparities of income reach down to the subsistence level. But the economic case made for this prediction of abundance is dubious, to say the least. Fortunately, Proudhon has a better argument for the relative acceptability of mutualist hierarchy. This one points out that productive contribution varies within narrow limits as compared to other criteria of distribution such as talent

---

by the greatest possible number of men," *Cont.*, II, 308.

Did Proudhon perhaps think that though abundance was good it was unattainable? Those who say this rely mainly on passages from *La guerre et la paix* like the following: "When you have done everything that energetic production and exact distribution allow to make yourselves rich, you will be astonished to see that you have actually done no more than earn your living, and that you haven't the resources to take a two week vacation." p. 336.

If an economy counts as abundant when it produces many more goods and services than are needed to support physical life, then Proudhon certainly thought abundance possible, despite passages like the foregoing. Misunderstanding has arisen because he uses the term "abundance" in an odd way, to denote a situation where more goods and services are produced than are consumed, *G.P.*, p. 242. It is this excess of production over consumption, and *not* a surplus of production over subsistence, that he thinks unattainable, *ibid.*, p. 343.

He may be as mistaken to say that every good and service produced must be consumed, as he would have been if he had said it is impossible to produce more goods and services than are needed to support physical life. But since he did not make the second statement, his prediction of abundance cannot be criticized as inconsistent with it.

So far as I know, Gaëtan Pirou is the only writer who remarks on Proudhon's odd definition of abundance. See *Proudhonisme et syndicalisme révolutionnaire* (Paris, 1910), p. 45.

and prestige. A mutualist hierarchy is therefore a rather shallow one.[47]

## The Consolations of Love

So firmly convinced was Proudhon of the need for the productivity standard to safeguard peace, that once he had made it a part of mutualism, he never again questioned it in principle. Nevertheless, he sensed its inconsistency with his highest value and tried to eliminate its most vicious consequences. These consequences affect anyone whose productive contribution is less than equivalent to his needs. Take the case of a father of a large family who is as efficient a producer as a bachelor. He will have far greater difficulty in executing his decisions and winning acceptance for them. Once "production and need are considered equivalent terms,"[48] those who rank low in productive contribution, or have especially high needs, will inevitably suffer disrespectful treatment.

In order to avoid the hardships and indignities imposed by the productivity standard, Proudhon suggests that the recognition and satisfaction of purposes, which mutualist society can only partially achieve, be completed within the family, in love relationships. This suggestion is supported by an analysis of family relations designed to prove that they cannot possibly be organized according to mutualist social principles.

Only relations among parties who exchange commensurable goods can be arranged on mutualist lines. If the goods offered by contenders cannot be assessed by the same standard, agreement on terms of trade cannot be

[47] *Justice*, III, 129.    [48] *I.G.*, p. 174.

achieved. Proudhon claims that the goods exchanged among members of a family have no such common measure. To back up this thesis he cites the example of a good offered by husbands—the ability to earn a living—and insists that it cannot be evaluated in terms of goods offered by wives, such as tenderness and the capacity to keep house. If these goods, and others like them, are intrinsically incommensurable, it certainly makes no sense to organize family relations on mutualist lines.[49]

How then should they be arranged? For obscure reasons, Proudhon says that within the family the only respectful relations are self-sacrificial ones. It is by offering one another unlimited devotion that members of a family defend pursuit of the distinctive ends sought in love relations and show understanding of them. Among kin, respect enjoins "complete sacrifice of the person, total abnegation of the self."[50]

Whatever the reasons for Proudhon's support of this form of family life, its effect is to alleviate mutualism's disrespectful treatment of inefficient producers. Anyone who does not make the grade in mutualist society can still win respect within the family by benefiting from his relatives' devotion. In public, he must endure harsh adversities, but if his family applies the same values as contenders in the way appropriate to its relationship with him, it can offer some of the respect that they withhold. His wife, for instance, will give him reward not proportional to his production, but to her unlimited love and devotion for him. She will give him more than he deserves.[51] By oblig-

[49] *Justice*, IV, 267, 271.    [50] *Justice*, IV, 278.    [51] *Ibid.*, IV, 274.

ing her to do so, respect, as applied to family life, "softens the sharp edges of Justice [and] destroys its asperities."[52]

It is easy to see that the sort of family relationship envisaged by Proudhon could compensate to some extent for the disrespect imposed by mutualist society, but could not avert it. An inept producer or a prolific father could not reach more satisfactory agreements on the strength of his family's tenderness, though its devotion might make his failure more tolerable. To make matters worse, it is precisely those most in need of familial devotion, the disadvantaged, who are least likely to receive it. The poor have so much to worry about that they have little time for cultivating tenderness.

The conclusion is obvious. Since a hierarchy degrades the members of Proudhon's ideal society, his scheme is a failure on its own terms. Despite all his efforts to remove it, a moral gap remains between his description of mutualism and the rules of respect.

### The Problem of Survival

Although Proudhon violates his basic values by building inequality into his ideal arrangements, this contradiction might be acceptable if it assured the survival of an otherwise respectful world. Unfortunately, mutualism is anything but stable.

One threat to the stability of mutualist society stems from its ineffectiveness in the world arena. Being stateless, it lacks the means to make and carry out a resolute foreign policy. It is therefore so handicapped in the conduct of

[52] *Ibid.*, IV, 270.

diplomacy and war as to be a prime target for aggressive rivals.[53]

Sometimes Proudhon meets this threat by denying its existence. The taproot of international belligerence is domestic conflict; states wage war to quell internal strife.[54] Hence, by ending domestic combat, mutualist social reorganization eliminates external aggression. Nations subscribing to mutualism simply do not indulge in warfare and so do not provoke retaliation from others.[55]

This solution to the external threat is inadequate if only because aggression is sometimes unprovoked. Even if mutualist societies were as outwardly pacific as Proudhon claims, they still might be attacked without provocation, by nations with a different form of internal organization. A mutualist society's national security thus requires that all nations be organized on mutualist lines. Proudhon sometimes sees this problem, but he evades it with professions of faith in the triumph of his ideal over "the entire surface of the globe."[56] In his early writings this confidence stems from faith in the exemplary power of mutualism. It is there portrayed as so advantageous that its establishment in any nation will convince all the others to adopt it.[57] But by the time he wrote the *Capacité*, Proudhon had stopped relying on the self-evident merits of his plan. In that work he rests his case for the world triumph of mutualism on the claim that it is invincible in defensive war.[58]

Proudhon's attempts to ward off the foreign threat to

[53] *I.G.*, p. 331.      [54] *G.P.*, p. 398.      [55] *Cap.*, p. 219.
[56] *Ibid.*, p. 220.      [57] *I.G.*, pp. 333-35.      [58] *Cap.*, pp. 219-20.

survival are so manifestly ineffective that the only points worth making about them are explanatory. The truth is that Proudhon did not think very hard about the international requisites for his domestic arrangements—at least while he was making them. His attention was drawn to the world arena only during the Italian War, in 1859, after he had completed *Justice*.[59] Though he did make some shrewd points about international affairs in his last years, they did nothing to build confidence in the durability of mutualism—quite the reverse. Hence it is hardly surprising that he coped so feebly with the foreign threat. At first he was scarcely aware of it; when its significance became apparent to him, he sensed that it was irresistible.

The internal threat to the survival of mutualism receives more serious attention. The problem here is that even if social pressure worked successfully, so that all members of society accepted the rules of respect as their highest norms and tried to apply them correctly, they might still think and act in ways forbidden by mutualist principles and practices. In other words the safe operation of a mutualist society requires more of its members than strict adherence to the rules of respect. These rules say nothing about how I, as a contender, should react to an adversary's claims and demands, since my obligation to respect another does not depend on his behavior toward me, but on "his being human." I owe unconditional respect to any man, even if he offers me nothing, but I cer-

[59] Nicolas Bourgeois, *Les théories de droit international chez Proudhon* (Paris, 1927), p. 21; Madeleine Amoudruz, *Proudhon et l'Europe* (Paris, 1945), p. 51.

tainly do not owe all my goods and services to people who offer me no compensation.[60] Mutualist society involves more complicated relations than this. The productivity standard, the norm of commutative justice, and the principles of social organization are all essential ingredients of mutualism that cannot be put into effect by respect's imperatives.

To close the gap between the rules of respect and the regulative needs of mutualism, Proudhon proposes to extend the influence of social pressure. Besides securing acceptance and application of his highest value, social pressure is also to win assent and compliance for mutualist principles and practices. This is to be achieved through a system of contracts.

The trouble with bargaining as actually practiced, so far as the survival of mutualism is concerned, is that it is conjectural and implicit. Terms are seldom expressly delineated by both sides and must usually be surmised by each.[61] In ordinary circumstances this inexplicitness does not matter much. But under mutualism, where so much of social life depends on bargaining, it is a major threat. If bargaining were conjectural there, the force of public opinion could not readily bear on it. Contenders could escape social censorship by keeping the terms of their agreements secret or vague and then would be free to make onerous deals.

To prevent this, Proudhon stipulates that agreement among mutualist contenders must be public, formal, and explicit. It must take the form of a "commutative con-

[60] *Justice*, I, 426.
[61] Chamberlain, pp. 265-69.

vention." "The act by which two or more individuals agree to partially and temporarily organize the industrial force we call exchange, and thereby bind themselves to reciprocally guarantee one another a certain sum of services, products, advantages, duties, etc., that they are in a position to procure and deliver."[62] Contenders who use such commutative conventions are less likely to make onerous deals than those who do not. For these conventions make agreement public and explicit, thereby exposing it to the control of social pressure.

But it is one thing to expose bargaining to social pressure and quite another to assure that this pressure exerts a salutary influence. The formalities suggested by Proudhon do not protect the integrity of bargaining. At most, they furnish a lever that might protect it if suitably manipulated. Proudhon understands very well that the mere requirement of convention-making does not accomplish much. In the "Cours" he reveals the full depth of his skepticism. "Who can oblige me to sign this convention, if I do not want to, if I find it to my advantage to keep my freedom of action? And if, after signing it, I break it, who can make my action criminal? What am I saying? Who will prove to me that I am the first to break it? When I prove that its conditions are leonine for me, that it is costly to me. . . . And then, who will be judge between me and my co-contractors? Who will decide between us?"[63] Though Proudhon's publications do not explicitly repeat these questions, they do try to answer them.

The fullest answer is found in *Justice*, where Proudhon

[62] *I.G.*, p. 188.
[63] *Cours*, I-14A (13), ellipsis in original.

puts his trust in family love. According to that work, family love can do more than soften the inequities of the productivity standard. If strong and constant, it can also furnish "the psychological conditions" for development of a mutualist frame of mind. For one thing, love produces a yearning for justice in the abstract: "The more I love, the more I will be afraid to displease, and, as a result, the more I will respect myself; now, the more vivid this self-respect becomes, the more strongly will I feel it sympathetically in others; and, consequently, the more just I will be."[64]

Such a disposition toward abstract justice is obviously inadequate for securing compliance with specific mutualist rules; at most it might win adherence to the norms of respect. But Proudhon claims something else for family love that gets around this difficulty. Love does more than stimulate a disposition toward justice in the abstract; it also "unceasingly directs" this disposition "from the abstract to the concrete."[65] By doing so, it wins assent and compliance for the principles and practices of mutualism.

Proudhon's claims for love greatly simplify the problem of applying mutualist principles, for they reduce it to the task of strengthening bonds of affection. If men's families can only be made to love them enough, Proudhon says in effect, then, in their roles as contenders, they will follow all the mutualist rules and will want everyone else to do the same. Social expectations will then arise that exert pressure on all opposed parties to shape their thought

[64] *Justice*, IV, 264.    [65] *Justice*, IV, 274.

and action into patterns compatible with mutualist requirements.

Proudhon offers scant evidence for these claims, and there is little reason to think them true. Hence the best verdict on his theory of family love is the one issued by Daniel Halévy, who once called the Proudhonian family "a mystical institution, the most astonishing of all."[66] It is indeed astonishing that Proudhon puts such a heavy reformative burden on an institution whose capacity for social reform is so strictly limited.

Suppose, nonetheless, for the sake of argument, that family love can create a disposition to follow mutualist rules. In that case, social pressure would in fact support the mental and behavioral patterns needed to make mutualist society safe and stable. But even then, the problem of survival would not be solved. Social pressure is too weak and too unreliable to preserve peace, even in Proudhon's ideal environment, where temptation to disobey social rules is weak, and opportunity seldom arises. Public opinion, no matter how loyal to the mutualist cause, will not always urge the safest course, because it is inherently vague, indiscriminate, and prone to excess.[67] Hence the threat of internal strife is never far away.

[66] *Journal des débats* (January 3, 1913). Halévy's description echoes Proudhon's in *Cont.*, ii, 198. Yet no less a writer than Georges Sorel singled out Proudhon's theory of love for special praise. *Reflections on Violence*, Collier Book edition (New York, 1961), p. 235.

[67] S. I. Benn and R. S. Peters, *Social Principles and the Democratic State* (London, 1959), pp. 230-33; George Orwell, "Politics vs. Literature: An Examination of Gulliver's Travels," reprinted in *The Orwell Reader*, ed. Richard Rovere (New York, 1956), pp. 292-93.

Nor should it be forgotten that control by public opinion is as much of an indignity as control by more readily identified coercive agents. Social pressures are better hidden than legal and political controls, but this does not make them less disrespectful. Though they may curb the individual's action less strictly, they can manipulate his will better than the more orthodox kinds of regulation. Through the process of internalization, they win better access to his inward thoughts and feelings. Hence Proudhon's reliance on public opinion to guarantee the survival of mutualism transforms it into a thoroughly disrespectful ideal, without securing its stability. Social pressure plays the same role in the reformative part of his theory as in his ethics. In both cases it violates first principles for the sake of their achievement, but without success. In other words, social pressure serves as a desperate realist's morally inadmissible last resort.

### *Two Types of Social Conformism:*
### *Marx and Proudhon*

Social pressure fails to solve Proudhon's problems; nothing else could solve them either. Any attempt to describe social arrangements that guarantee both personal security and observance of respect is bound to fail, because these aims cannot be simultaneously attained. Nevertheless, it may be that within the limits imposed by the futility of his search, Proudhon reached a relatively favorable compromise between peace and respect. That he did is suggested by a comparison of his recommendations with those of Marx.

Marx's classless, stateless society has a purpose similar

to Proudhon's mutualist society. It too aims at securing peace and freedom without resort to government and hierarchy. The method Marx uses to stabilize his ideal society is like Proudhon's; he too uses social pressure. But Marx's way of using social pressure leaves less room for freedom than Proudhon's, without making peace any more secure.

It is clear even from Marx's rough sketch of the classless society that social pressure plays a greater role in his ideal arrangements than in Proudhon's. Under communism occurs "the genuine resolution of the conflict . . . between man and man." "That which I make of myself, I make of myself for society."[68] Social pressure, as conceived by Marx, molds decisions so thoroughly that disagreement about the aims of conduct does not arise. Under mutualism too, social pressure instills a good deal of agreement on objectives, but less than under communism. Although Proudhon is careful to stress that consensus on his system's fundamental principles must prevail, he gives equal emphasis to the large margin for disagreement on circumstantials that remains. The monolithic agreement envisaged by Marx strikes him as fitting only in a primitive community, where blind custom is the sole form of social control. Among the civilized and, a fortiori, under mutualism, disagreement is permissible on all questions except those covered by fundamental norms.

The abolition of conflicting aspirations under communism ends behavioral conflict too. In the classless society men all act the same way or, at most, in compatible ways.

[68] Karl Marx, *Economic and Philosophic Manuscripts of 1844*, trans., Martin Milligan (Moscow, 1961), pp. 102, 104.

In Aristotle's metaphor, they all either sound the same note, or else different notes in the same key.[69] It is true that action is also harmonious under mutualism. "Corporative forces balance, and through their just equilibrium, produce general happiness. The opposition of forces thus has their harmony as its end."[70] But mutualist harmony is less confining than that produced by communism. Although behavior is concordant, it is not a "concert of instruments in tune like the pipes of an organ," much less a playing in unison.[71] People need not refrain from pursuing incompatible objectives, but may discuss and bargain until they reach mutually satisfactory terms of agreement. For Proudhon, therefore, social pressure does not abolish conflict in order to bring about harmony, as it does for Marx. Instead, it limits conflict so that people can arrive at agreements, but, within these limits, leaves them free to seek incompatible ends.

Proudhon even goes a step further to insist that appropriately limited conflict is desirable. "Diversities are the very basis . . . of mutualism."[72] He was no advocate of agreement for its own sake because he thought that anything more than a minimal consensus was unduly repressive. One of the things most needed by his ideal man

[69] Aristotle, *Politics*, ed. Ernest Barker (New York, 1958), p. 51.

[70] *G.P.*, p. 134.

[71] *Justice*, III, 405.

[72] *Cap.*, p. 218. Marx explicitly denounced Proudhon's celebration of conflict. See the interesting confrontation by Robert C. Tucker, "Marx and Distributive Justice" in *Justice*, eds. Carl J. Friedrich and John W. Chapman (New York, 1963), pp. 324-25.

is "that bellicose disposition which puts him above all authority."[73]

This qualified defense of conflict is entirely in keeping with Proudhon's belief that the good society is based on bargaining and discussion. Both of these are by nature at once cooperative and antagonistic activities.[74] They begin in conflict and end in consensus. Hence, in a society like Proudhon's, where bargaining and discussion prevail, rivalry and agreement are equally necessary. "Whoever speaks of harmony and agreement" in such a society "necessarily assumes conflicting terms," for then "there has to be a struggle before there can be a settlement."[75]

The presence of bargaining and discussion in Proudhon's ideal society, and their absence from Marx's, is thus the point that explains the main differences between them. Marx relied exclusively on the pressure of public opinion to protect the stability endangered by the absence of law and government. By doing so, he was obliged to inject a strong dose of social pressure into his system. Proudhon, on the other hand, relied on bargaining and discussion as well as social pressure. His use of the former allowed him to lean less heavily on the latter in his effort to secure peace. For him, social pressure had to enforce only a fundamental agreement beyond which conflicts of interest and ideals, though not of basic values, were given

[73] *G.P.*, p. 464. To preclude misunderstanding, it should be noted that Proudhon was no advocate of conflict for its own sake. "Antagonism has no value except by virtue of the creation of which it is the agent," *G.P.*, p. 477.

[74] Chamberlain, *General Theory of Economic Process*, pp. 77-78, 85.

[75] *Justice*, III, 256; *G.P.*, p. 54.

free reign. Within the framework of mutualist principles people were allowed to choose as well as act as they saw fit. It is easily seen that Proudhon's reliance on bargaining does more than account for the differences between his ideal and Marx's. It also explains why it is more respectful. By giving people more leeway to act and resolve as they please, mutualism comes closer than communism to adherence to respect's imperatives.

### From Mutualism to Federalism

Whatever its advantages over Marx's ideal, the fact remains that mutualism was, and had to be, a failure on its own terms, because the problems that face it are insoluble. The only way Proudhon could hope to frame successful proposals was to admit that he had been asking the wrong questions. At the very end of his life he did just that. As late as 1860 he was still berating "the principle of authority as incompatible with man's dignity."[76] He still wanted to achieve respect absolutely. But just three years later he admitted that his arch-enemy was invincible and that perfect adherence to the rules of respect could not be achieved. "Liberty . . . assumes an Authority that bargains with it, restrains it, tolerates it. . . . It follows that in any society, . . . even the most liberal, a place is reserved for Authority."[77] Once Proudhon had admitted this, a new way of putting the problem of social reconstruction came into sight. He no longer asked, How

[76] *Justice*, II, 311. But cf. IV, 456, written just a few months after the foregoing, where signs of reconciliation with authority are already apparent.
[77] P.F., pp. 271-72.

can perfect order and respect be achieved? but How can society be arranged so as to achieve as much of each as possible? The ideals that he had once sought to realize were now "condemned permanently to the status of desiderata."[78] The problem was to "balance Authority with Liberty and vice versa," not to destroy the first and perfectly achieve the other.[79]

What this meant in more concrete terms was that in the end Proudhon accepted the need for government. He did more than accept it; he went on to show how its disrespectful effects could be minimized. This demonstration involved elaboration of one of his best-known doctrines: his theory of federalism.

As Franz Neumann has noted, Proudhon's "theory of federalism has nothing in common with that of the federal state; it is rather the very negation of it."[80] The sharp distinction between Proudhon's federalism and the more orthodox varieties results from a difference of underlying purpose. Most advocates of federation have supported their case with strictly political arguments. Either they see federalism as a way to divide power without impairing its effectiveness too much; or they point to its encouragement of grass-roots political participation; or else they emphasize its usefulness for bringing a diverse population under a common government. In short, they back federalism as a way toward constitutionalism, democracy, or unity. Proudhon's defense is quite different. He supports fed-

[78] *Ibid.*, p. 279; cf. *Corr.*, XII, 220-21, letter of Dec. 2, 1862.
[79] *Ibid.*, p. 272.
[80] Franz Neumann, *The Democratic and the Authoritarian State* (Glencoe, 1957), p. 218.

eralism not for the sake of its political effects, but as a political arrangement that can protect mutualist social practices with minimal resort to governmental authority. Unless it is understood that Proudhon's federalism has this unorthodox objective, many of its most curious features remain obscure.[81]

No more than the briefest description of these features is needed here. While recognizing that excessive dismantling of central government is dangerous, Proudhon is anxious to go far in this direction.[82] The fact that mutualism enables society to perform many functions without governmental assistance allows him to go a considerable distance. His federalism is a contractual arrangement in which the largest units are assigned the fewest powers and the smallest ones the most. The result is the subordination of the higher levels to the lower. The local units are even given the right to secede. For Proudhon a federal state is one "whose parties, recognized as sovereign, have the choice of leaving the group and breaking the pact *ad libitum*."[83]

From this description it looks as if Proudhon goes further toward dismantling government than even the most enthusiastic economic liberals, for though they favored a non-interventionist state, they wanted it to be strong within its limited sphere. This inference is not strictly correct. Though Proudhon does not assign all of the

[81] Stanley Hoffmann calls attention to just this feature of Proudhon's federalism. See "The Areal Division of Powers in the Writings of French Political Thinkers" in *Area and Power*, ed. Arthur Maass (Glencoe, 1959), p. 129.
[82] *P.F.*, p. 355.     [83] *Cap.*, p. 207.

powers to central government that the liberals do, he nevertheless gives it others that they withhold. True, the Proudhonian central government is an imperfect night watchman, since it is not given much power to police the bargaining process. But it also plays another, more positive, role. It is a creative initiator as well as a neutral arbiter and enforcer. "The State is the generator and supreme director of movement. . . . [It] is always in action, because it continually has new needs to satisfy, new questions to resolve."[84] The only thing the central government emphatically is *not* is a routine administrator. "After introducing an innovation, . . . the State withdraws, leaving execution of the new service to local authorities and citizens."[85] Proudhonian federalism is thus far from opposed to intervention from the center, though it is incompatible with centralized administration.

It is not hard to show that federalism is a closer approximation of Proudhon's social ideal than mutualism. Admittedly, neither arrangement is more respectful than the other. Both include principles which, being hierarchic, are incompatible with Proudhon's supreme values. Both try to secure obedience to these principles by equally disrespectful means. Social pressure manipulates decisions, instead of identifying with them. Law and government coerce action, instead of leaving it unrestrained.

But though federalism is no more respectful than mutualism, it is better able to maintain order. In principle, certainly, law and government are more reliable methods of social control than public opinion. Hence there is a strong presumption that federalism is a more stable sys-

[84] *P.F.*, pp. 327, 329.      [85] *Ibid.*, p. 327.

tem than mutualism. It might be objected, however, that this presumption does not hold for Proudhon's federalism, because there central government is so thoroughly dismembered that it cannot effectively manage conflict. To this objection two answers are possible. The first is a reminder that Proudhon's federal government is designed to regulate no ordinary society, but a mutualist one. He is perfectly willing to admit that a federation of the kind he advocates could not maintain order in any actual societies. But a mutualist society is organized according to principles which dispose its members to resolve their disputes peacefully. Under these conditions, Proudhon argues, a government assigned no more than the jobs he gives it is an adequate instrument for maintaining peace.[86]

Should the objector remain unconvinced, Proudhon could retreat to a second, less explicit, line of defense. He is not so much interested in prescribing a fixed and ideal pattern for the territorial distribution of power, as in calling attention to some general principles for its allocation. The book in which he outlines his scheme is about the federative *principle*, and is intended to put us "on the road to truth," not lay down the final word.[87] Hence, though Proudhon's specific recipe for allocating power may dismantle central government too much, there is nothing in his general theory of federalism to prevent more centralization, should it be needed to maintain peace.

Is federalism, judged by Proudhon's own standards, superior not only to mutualism, but to all existing, more unitary governmental arrangements? If suitably adjusted, federalism can perhaps protect personal security as well,

[86] *Ibid.*, p. 330; cf. *Cap.*, p. 211.
[87] *P.F.*, p. 326.

though certainly no better than more centralized plans. Hence it may be as good a maintainer of order as they, at least potentially. But since it is at best only on a par with them as a manager of conflict, it must excel as an achiever of respect, if it is to qualify as superior in Proudhon's eyes. Certainly, Proudhon's federation restrains action less severely than more centralized governments. But it more frequently manipulates the will. Judged by the norms of respect, then, Proudhon's final plan for social reconstruction is no improvement on existing arrangements. Federalism may allow more freedom of action, but this advantage is offset by its more frequent disregard for personal choice.

## Bargaining and the Problem of Liberation

Although federalism falls at least as short of Proudhon's ideals as do unitary governments, it comes closer to them than mutualism. Nevertheless, it would be a mistake to dismiss the latter as utterly worthless. The truth is that federalism is indebted to the insights of mutualism for its superiority. Had Proudhon not first tried to describe a society of pure bargainers, totally liberated from government and hierarchy, he could scarcely have found the safe way to limited freedom from their control that he ultimately proposed. His theory of bargaining, though developed as part of mutualism, is thus crucial for federalism. It is the ingredient that excuses the failure of the former and explains the latter's relative success. Bargaining is the factor responsible for whatever reduction in political coercion federalism showed how to achieve.

Proudhon's insights into the nature of bargaining stem from his ambivalent view of it. He is both critical and enthusiastic. His enthusiasm for bargaining is aroused by its liberating potential, as we have seen. This practice is a promising alternative to the market, hierarchy, and law for anyone who despises "presumptive authority" and wants "to handle matters directly, individually, by himself."[88] Such a person sees all existing societies as hopelessly contaminated by higher authorities who overrule opposed parties instead of letting them resolve their disputes by themselves.

Though Proudhon was one of the first to denounce established institutions on this ground, he was certainly not the last. A long line of pluralists have sung the praise of bargaining for similar reasons. But seldom have they done so with much recognition of that practice's dangers. This was not the case with Proudhon. His fear of a Hobbesian nightmare led him to discover some, but by no means all, of the social and psychological conditions needed to make bargaining operate successfully. His theory of bargaining may therefore serve as a suggestive starting point for anyone who wants to complete the unfinished search for these conditions.

Just as Proudhon's realistic doubts led to an analysis of the prerequisites to bargaining, so his moral qualms inspired an investigation of its ethical validity. Here too a critical attitude distinguishes his view of bargaining from that of most advocates, who often assume, without much argument, that it is morally justified. One recent opponent has put the ethical case against it well: "To approach decision in the bargaining spirit is to confuse 'solving' with 'getting.' This confusion is part of the pathology of the

[88] *I.G.*, p. 211.

governing process . . . [which] . . . is a cooperative not a competitive activity and, in spirit, utterly alien to the bargaining temper of the marketplace."[89] With much of this critique, Proudhon agrees completely. Bargainers left free to follow an unchecked course are all too likely to choose a disrespectful one. But unlike the critics who make this point Proudhon does not prescribe a legalistic remedy by empowering neutral third parties to judge disputes. Bargaining has a liberating promise as well as a disrespectful one. The proper course is therefore not to scrap it but to perfect it by appropriate techniques of moral regulation. If contenders all accept the same standards of justice, there will be no need for higher authorities to impose settlements. Disputes will then be resolved safely and equitably by the interested parties themselves.

Proudhon certainly comes no nearer to moralizing bargaining than to stabilizing it. The value of his position lies more in its intention than its accomplishment. But in the process of imperfectly developing his position, he dropped hints of its unrealized possibilities, thus inviting its revival and further elaboration in times to come. In spite of the present popularity of bargaining, no one has yet devised a satisfactory theory, fully elucidating its requirements, advantages, and limitations.[90] Proudhon's approach to these questions may be of use, as both a model and a warning, to those who continue the enterprise he helped begin.

[89] Joseph Tussman, *Obligation and the Body Politic* (New York, 1960), p. 117. This is one of the book's most insistent but least adequately defended points; cf. pp. 30, 71-2, 81, 99, 115-16.

[90] Dahl and Lindblom lament that "bargaining lacks a widely accepted theoretical rationale." *Politics, Economics and Welfare*, p. 472.

# CHAPTER VI

## Tactical Problems: The Disparity
## Between Means and Ends

I N matters of reform, it is not ordinarily the objective that is lacking, or the will to reach it, but the means."[1] Proudhon directs this charge at his adversaries, but it also applies to him, for one of the most striking features of his theory is the disparity between its ambitious ends and the impotent methods relied on to attain them.

The cause of this disparity is Proudhon's perfectionist attitude toward his highest norms. So valuable are the rules of respect that they must apply to means no less than to ends. The path to freedom and justice must also be free and just. Hence tactics for achieving mutualism must be judged "strictly from the viewpoint of principle, . . . never after the event, from the viewpoint of success."[2] What this purism entails in practice is avoidance of the tactics most favored by radical reformers, such as violence, propaganda, and legislation. These tactics are all strictly forbidden by respect's imperatives; only the mildest and most conciliatory are sanctioned.[3]

If his perfectionist rigor explains why Proudhon chose moderate strategies, the situation he faced accounts for

---

[1] *Justice*, III, 56.   [2] *Mel.*, II, 59.

[3] *Carnets*, III, 106. "No authority is compatible with the principle of mutuality, but no authority can help bring about reform. For all authority is antithetical to equality and justice."

their impotence. The fact is that prevailing conditions doom efforts to achieve mutualism by scrupulously respectful means. Such efforts might conceivably succeed if they did not provoke hostility. But the mutualist program is so controversial that it is bound to arouse vigorous opposition. In the face of such resistance, the moderate tactics prescribed by respect cannot possibly succeed.

## *The Varieties of Perfectionist Impotence*

Though Proudhon consistently put his trust in moderate tactics, he did not always espouse the same ones. On the contrary, the record of his strategic thought shows him restlessly turning from one tactic to another in a vain search for one that would meet both the imperatives of respect and a growing appreciation of the obstacles to mutualist reform.

At the beginning of his career Proudhon showed little awareness of strategic difficulties. As he then viewed the problem of reform, the only bar was ignorance. Hence it is not surprising that in his first writings his perfectionist impulse is allowed free reign. He relied exclusively on an especially pure kind of education for the attainment of his ends. "Stimulate, warn, inform, instruct, but do not inculcate," he prescribed.[4] Inculcation had to be avoided because use of threats, rewards, or psychological conditioning was morally inadmissible; it was also strategically unnecessary, because rational education was psychologically compelling. Once men had been exposed to his principles, Proudhon then believed, they could be counted on to apply them. "Wherever this discourse is read or

[4] *Ibid.*, vi, 269; cf. *Justice*, i, 227.

made known, . . . there privilege and servitude will sooner or later disappear."[5]

No tactic could be more respectful than rational education; but none could be more impotent. So long as Proudhon relied solely on compelling knowledge to attain his ends, he was sure not to reach them. In the *Contradictions* he still counted on the salutary effects of education, but his appreciation of the obstacles to reform was growing.[6] Hence, while he still used moral principles to certify the measures he prescribed, he also tried to show the futility of the palliative reforms that were then the main alternative to a perfectionist strategy. Since the other options are tactically hopeless, he argues in effect, the wise choice is to stick with measures that are at least morally pure. The relevance of the *Contradictions* for tactics thus lies far more in its attack on rival strategies than in its defense of Proudhon's. It is a *locus classicus* for subsequent arguments against meliorism.

The book's main strategic point is that "the needs of the established order" preclude all attempts at palliative reform. "Society can only subsist at that price."[7] Under existing conditions, some palliatives have the exact opposite of their intended effect; instead of improving the lot of the oppressed, they make it worse. Schemes to give workers control of industry, for instance, are meant to raise income, but would in fact lower it, for in the long run they would reduce entrepreneurial skill and thus diminish

[5] *Prop.*, p. 345.
[6] *Cont.*, II, 406; but cf. *Corr.*, II, 257, where, in a letter of 1842, Proudhon already expresses doubts about the power of knowledge.
[7] *Cont.*, I, 323.

productivity.[8] Proudhon sees the same short-coming in price and wage controls. They deprive the economy of the flexibility it needs for rapid economic growth.[9]

Another palliative, the progressive income tax, is ruled out for a more subtle reason. Although this measure might increase the incomes of the oppressed, it would reduce their ultimate chances for liberation by committing them to the status quo. The progressive income tax "makes taxation a kind of privilege for the privileged; a bad idea, because it gives de facto recognition to the legitimacy of privilege, which in no case, and in no form, is worth a thing."[10] Savings banks have a similar effect; they give the oppressed a tangible stake in the hierarchic order, thereby weakening their hostility to it.[11]

A final example of a subtly conservative kind of palliative is the public nursery for working mothers. In a sense this institution is even more insidious than progressive taxes and savings banks, because it alters the basic character of those it benefits. The administrators of such nurseries, by limiting their services to mothers "who behave properly," put a premium on the sort of docile character that suits the privileged classes.[12] Here Proudhon has provided the gist of an argument against welfare policies that continues to be heard in our own day. The welfare worker and his partisans may regard themselves as benefactors of the poor, but the effect of their activity is to reconcile the unprivileged to their lot by inducing them to adopt the bourgeois outlook of their superiors.

The outbreak of revolution in 1848 caused a major re-

[8] *Ibid.*, I, 148, 196.    [9] *Ibid.*, I, 201.    [10] *Ibid.*, I, 295.
[11] *Ibid.*, II, 152.    [12] *Ibid.*, II, 145.

vision in Proudhon's tactics. As is well known, he greeted the events of that year with consternation. One source of his dismay was dislike for the revolutionaries who, perhaps unavoidably, violated his highest principles. But Proudhon was less concerned to criticize the men who had seized power than to expose critics on the left—mainly Victor Considérant, Louis Blanc and Auguste Blanqui —who proposed a different revolutionary strategy from the one actually followed. Considérant, who hoped to revolutionize the world with model communities, is condemned for needing "minds to experiment on, which he may mould as he sees fit." Such moulding of personality is forbidden by a perfectionist application of respect's imperatives. "What! You want to increase men's freedom . . . and yet, as a precondition to the happiness you promise them, you ask them to surrender their bodies, their souls, their minds, their traditions, their goods, to put their entire being into your hands! But who are you to substitute your limited wisdom for eternal reason?"[13] Blanc's welfare state is also easy to condemn from this point of view. "As he writes himself, he needs dictatorial authority to improve the world."[14] It matters little that the administrators of the welfare state would be popularly elected. They would still impose restrictions on action and choice. Reform "must have everyone as author and accomplice"; otherwise, it is disrespectful. Nor does Blanc's plan to nationalize industry legitimize his tactics. If you substitute government for private ownership, "nothing is changed but the stockholders and the management; beyond that, there

[13] *Conf.*, pp. 252-53.    [14] *Ibid.*, p. 252.

— 167 —

is not the least difference in the position of the workers."[15] The same criticism holds even more strongly for a Blanquist dictatorship. Blanqui's strategy is "a glorification of force. It is the theory of all governments turned against the governing classes; the problem of tyrannical majorities resolved in favor of the workers, as it is today in favor of the bourgeoisie."[16] If Blanc is wrong to oppress minorities, then Blanqui is all the more culpable, since he proposes to oppress majorities.

But if Proudhon was to further the mutualist cause, he had to do more than criticize his opponents' tactics. He had to find some path to reform that was a viable alternative to coercive change. The method of rational education was now too obviously insufficient to recommend; events were moving too rapidly and opposition was too strong for the slightest chance of success. The device Proudhon turned to as a substitute for education under revolutionary conditions was the *Banque du peuple*, his free credit scheme. To prove its merits, he made the two points one would expect. He argued that it was both respectful and effective.

His case for the respectfulness of the Bank is easy to accept. No one would be compelled to do business there, while those who did would not obstruct abstainers in any way. Hence the Bank "interferes with no legitimate interest, it menaces no liberty."[17]

Proudhon's proof of the Bank's effectiveness is harder to grant. By 1848 he no longer saw ignorance as the major

[15] *Mel.*, III, 118.    [16] *Carnets*, IX, 2.
[17] *Conf.*, p. 252; cf. *Mel.*, II, 43.

bar to reform. He now believed that "men, unlike speculative philosophers, are motivated not by pure love of beauty and justice, but by their interests."[18] Hence the Bank's capacity to build mutualism depended on proof that it was profitable to those it affected rather than that it was good for them. Such proof is difficult to adduce. Proudhon's attempt consists of a social analysis purporting to show that only a small segment of the population had an interest in opposing the Bank, and that this segment can be dealt with by respectful means.

That the Bank would profit both the workers and the commercial middle class was self-evident, at least to Proudhon. "No opposition to revolutionary measures can arise from that quarter."[19] The only class that would find the Bank unprofitable were bourgeois "holders of government bonds, usurers, . . . and big property owners."[20] This class was neither numerous nor vigorous enough to block free credit, once the workers and the middle class had begun organizing it. Hence it could be left undisturbed. As the Bank's depositors grew in number, the bourgeoisie would be convinced "by a sense of the inevitable and concern for its interests, to voluntarily change the employment of its capital, unless it preferred to run the risk of consuming it unproductively and enduring swift and total ruin as a result."[21] The one group opposed to free credit would be overcome without infringing on its right to respect in any way.

This social analysis was defective on several scores: because it underrated the power of the bourgeoisie, exag-

[18] *Corr.*, III, 97.    [19] *R.S.*, p. 206.    [20] *Mel.*, III, 123.
[21] *R.S.*, p. 206.

gerated that of the commercial middle class, described as the "mainspring of progress," and because it portrayed the workers and the middle class as sharing common interests. All of these errors made Proudhon's image of French society much too consensual. It is true that in France at this time industrialization had just begun, so that the power of capitalists and the conflict between the commercial middle class and the workers were not yet fully apparent. But the June Days had already entered history; the new pattern of social relations was clear enough. Proudhon's failure to point it out is a symptom of his tactical preoccupations. His appreciation of the opposition to reform had grown. He had therefore come to doubt that tactics forceful enough to achieve mutualism could conform to the rules of respect. Yet he was unwilling to resort to measures at odds with his moral scruples. Hence his only option was to distort his analysis of social reality so as to make it appear more favorable to his enterprise than it was in fact.

Even if Proudhon's social analysis had proved that everyone except a few bourgeoisie would benefit from the Bank, it would not have explained how the Bank could reconstruct society on mutualist lines. To show that it could not possibly have this effect, one need only consider its general mode of operation. The Bank was to conduct two sorts of business: it would exchange commodities for an equivalent sum of money, and it would issue interest-free loans. The suppression of the "royauté de l'argent" achieved by these activities was supposed to end economic oppression and inequality, thus making government unnecessary and paving the way to total mutualist reform.[22] In Proudhon's intoxicated words, the Bank was "the solvent of all authority," which would "change the basis of society, shift the axis of civilization."[23]

Numerous technical objections have been raised to this scheme. Laissez-faire economists have pointed out that if the Bank's administrators took risks, the result would be inflationary; if they were cautious, the Bank could not produce its intended effects. Marxists have shown that even if the Bank operated as Proudhon hoped, it could not possibly remedy the profound causes of economic inequality, whose source was in the labor, not the money, market. It is even more noteworthy that the Bank, being a strictly monetary device, could have little effect on the forces Proudhon finds at the root of oppression, such as deference and law, yet these are the very forces he presumably intended to control. It is because he expected preposterously important results from a rather trivial institution that Proudhon has rightly acquired a reputation as a "money crank."

No doubt, in 1849, after his plans for the Bank had collapsed, Proudhon took a more modest view of its purpose. In retrospect he saw it as a prototype of fully developed mutualism, designed to prove its merits and diffuse its principles. It was to "prepare for political reform by an example of spontaneous centralization."[24] This more sober appraisal of the Bank does nothing to release Prou-

[22] Charles Gide and Charles Rist, *Histoire des doctrines économiques* (7th ed., Paris, 1947), I, 344.
[23] *Carnets*, VII, 203; *Mel.*, II, I.
[24] *Conf.*, p. 247.

dhon from the charge of exaggerating its effects. Both when he expected extravagant results from the Bank, and when, with hindsight, his hopes became more modest, he claimed that its establishment would lead to mutualism. This claim cannot withstand serious examination. Like his distorted analysis of social forces, his excessive hopes for the Bank have their source in the need to convince himself and others that respectful tactics can really achieve mutualism.

Proudhon did not give up economic gadgets until 1855.[25] The opening of the Universal Exposition in that year occasioned a *Projet d'exposition perpétuelle* that adapted his ideas about free credit to current events. But his remarks on strategy in the "Cours," which also date from this period, show that the tactics he was suggesting in private are free of the technical defects that encumber his published ones. The "Cours" says little about free credit, but contains a curious scheme for a "dictatorship by the people of Paris," apparently designed to reconstruct society forcibly on mutualist lines. By calling this tactic a dictatorship, Proudhon suggests that it is the exact opposite of the one he was publicly favoring at this time. In his unpublished writing, it appears, he recognized that intractable opposition compelled resort to disrespectful tactics, even at the cost of moral compromise.

The exacting preconditions imposed by the "Cours" to make a dictatorship permissible show that this is not the case. According to that work, a dictatorship is only permissible if "the people in triumph—I say 'the people'

[25] Edouard Dolléans, *Proudhon* (Paris, 1948), pp. 286-87.

because I assume that the bourgeoisie voluntarily withdraw—knows what its problem is, understands its cause, and therefore its cure, . . . and is resolved to use this cure."[26] In other words, those who hold power must apply mutualist principles, and no one must object to their doing so. However, the establishment of mutualism under such conditions hardly counts as dictatorial, under any ordinary meaning of that word. On the contrary, dictatorship as described in the "Cours" is an eminently respectful tactic, since it could interfere with no man's conduct or choice. Hence, despite appearances, the strategy Proudhon privately supported in the early 1850's was consistent with the one he was espousing in public. Though the "dictatorship" is unencumbered by the technical flaws that impair free credit, it is just as respectful and, consequently, just as impotent.

1855 marks a turning point in Proudhon's approach to strategy. He then decided that the major bar to reform was not personal interest after all, but moral error. To devise a strategy that profited everyone was not sufficient and perhaps not even necessary for the attainment of mutualism. What was needed was a transformation of man's conscience. "The real object" of a search for adequate tactics became forcefully and thoroughly "to examine . . . the *moral question*."[27] The outcome of this endeavor was *De la Justice*, whose program is summarized in its announcement that "it is the disposition of consciences that must be changed."[28]

Proudhon's new concern with ethics had a strong im-

[26] "Cours" I-14D' (75).    [27] *Corr.*, VI, 175.
[28] *Justice*, IV, 476.

pact on his strategy. For one thing, it led to disenchantment with monetary devices. Now the ethical effects of free credit seemed most important, although at the time he had favored it, it was its effect on personal interest that he had stressed. "Behind my ardent polemics there lay thoughts of moral renovation more than a theory of political economy," he now maintained.[29] Proudhon's turn toward ethics also affected his strategic thought more positively by inspiring a return to education as a way to mutualism. In its revived form, Proudhonian education was more moral and less technical than it had been. It concentrated on the basic principles of mutualism, not the details of its practice. Along with this shift in strategy from concern with interests to concern with ethics went a clearer vision of the obstacles to successful reform. No longer did Proudhon delude himself with a rosy but false social analysis of the prospects for mutualism. Nor did he persist in overestimating the reformative power of education. "The conversion of societies is never sudden. ... It is assured, but one must know how to wait for it."[30] While remaining convinced that education would ultimately secure the triumph of his ideal, Proudhon no longer hoped for its prompt realization. All one could do was teach and wait. As he aptly said, his tactical stance had become that of "attente révolutionnaire."[31]

In view of the hopelessness of this strategy, it is not surprising that in his last years Proudhon was pessimistic about the prospects for his enterprise. In April 1859 he confided to one of his closest friends: "Discouragement

[29] Cited in Dolléans, p. 286.     [30] *Justice*, IV, 489.
[31] *Ibid.*, IV, 468.

overtakes me bit by bit as I witness the stupidity and dishonesty of mankind. My juvenile indignation of former times is wearing out; with greater lucidity of mind, inertia gets hold of me and I become sad. I see nothing that will defeat this troublesome disposition except serious long-term studies addressed to the future and another generation."[32] Despite his hopelessness, Proudhon put his trust in moral education until almost the end of his life. In 1863, however, the turn of events, abetted by the sting of pessimism, suggested a new strategy, which comes closer than any other he recommended to allying respectfulness with potency. This new strategy is worked out in *De la capacité politique des classes ouvrières.*

Two events occasioned it. The first was the legislative election of 1863. For the first time in the history of the Second Empire a majority of the Parisian voters withdrew their support from the official candidates and backed the legal opposition. Proudhon observed that many of those who had turned against the official slate were workers, and he drew a conclusion of the highest consequence. Until 1863, he pointed out, the votes of the workers had been a mere "imitation of bourgeois votes, or rather, a supplement to them." But in the election of that year, the workers finally "asserted their will and character."[33] By doing so, they suggested to Proudhon that they might be a more effective instrument for achieving mutualism than he had previously thought.

Another event strengthened his confidence in the proletariat. An important by-election was held in Paris in 1864.

[32] *Corr.,* IX, 71, to Chaudey.     [33] *Cap.,* pp. 61, 72.

In anticipation, a number of workers, led by Henri To-
lain, published a manifesto urging their comrades to
nominate candidates of their own class, rather than vote
for those of the legal opposition, as they had in 1863.
Proudhon enthusiastically praised the manifesto as further evidence of the workers' developing sense of class
solidarity. Its writers "faced the situation that events and
the law had imposed on them, and they spoke from the
depths of their working class consciousness."[34]

One trouble with Proudhon's new assessment of the
proletariat was that it disagreed with the social analysis
he had made in 1848 to support his scheme for free credit.
Then he had called the proletariat a passive adjunct of
the commercial middle class. The events of 1863-1864 led
him to revise this analysis in a way that not only confirmed his new trust in the workers but drew a more accurate picture of social reality.

The same three classes figure in Proudhon's revised
analysis of society as in his old one: bourgeois capitalists,
commercial middle class, and proletariat. Their mutual
relations are also the same. The bourgeoisie is portrayed
as hostile to a proletariat and a middle class that are potential allies. Where the new analysis differs from the old
is in its ascription of power to the three groups. The workers now appear as an ascending, self-reliant class, rather
than as the dependent clients previously described. The
bourgeoisie is also recognized for what it is: not a troublesome but insignificant minority, which would disappear without protest if only its opponents would unite, but

[34] *Ibid.*, p. 96.

a strong and united elite, "which is rich, which dominates, which has know-how and power."[35] As for the middle class of artisans, shopkeepers, and small businessmen, it is demoted from its place as leader in the fight for mutualism to that of a passive follower. "The middle class is being slowly smothered, attacked head on by rising wages and the development of private corporations, and on its flanks by taxes and foreign competition, or free trade. It will ultimately be replaced by officialdom, the bourgeoisie and the wage-earning class."[36]

The heightened realism of this analysis is evident. Proudhon has deleted from his picture of society many of the features that once made it too consensual. What was formerly a harmonious society, under the improbable leadership of the commercial middle class, is now a conflicting one, with rival bourgeoisie and proletariat vying for predominance.

One further aspect of Proudhon's amended social analysis is noteworthy. In the *Capacité* he devotes special attention to the peasantry, a group he had previously ignored. Since the farmers live at the margin of industrial society, he now says, they have special aims, which set them apart from other classes. The peasant "wants to rule alone over his land," as a yeoman farmer, and so is hostile to the entire urban population, rich or poor, which he associates with absentee ownership.[37] By making this point about the peasantry, Proudhon adds another note of realism to his analysis. His completed picture of society has a place for the conflict between urban and rural, as well as between upper and lower classes.

[35] *Ibid.*, p. 100.     [36] *Ibid.*, p. 230.     [37] *Ibid.*, pp. 67-68.

Reference to the social facts, which this picture is meant to describe, underlines its accuracy. In France, the peasantry was then, and still is today, a larger and more independent group than in most Western countries. To ignore it is to distort one's image of reality. In France too, the commercial middle class carries its sympathies unusually far to the left. Hence Proudhon's hope that the middle class would ally with the workers was better warranted in the French context than it would have been in many others.

The implications for tactics of this new analysis are straightforward. To begin with, it offers positive proof that no free credit scheme can possibly succeed. Since the bourgeoisie is now described as large and strong, the *Banque du peuple*, which does not benefit this class, would not appeal to the interests of the vast majority. On the contrary, it would intensify class rivalry by augmenting conflict between the bourgeoisie and the rest of the population.[38] What is called for now, according to Proudhon, is a campaign that rallies the peasantry, the workers and the middle class remnant to the mutualist cause. Otherwise, mutualism cannot possibly secure the wide popular support needed for its triumph. The leaders of this new alliance can be none but the workers. They alone come close to having what Proudhon calls political capacity, for they have two of the traits that characterize it: they are aware of themselves as a class whose fortunes depend on common action, and they also understand the objectives of mutualism.[39] The middle class lacks both of these

[38] *Ibid.*, p. 239.   [39] *Ibid.*, p. 91.

qualifications; the peasants have only the first. Not even the workers have the final qualification: they "have not yet succeeded in deducing a correct overall practice and an appropriate policy from these [mutualist] principles."[40] Though they want to act in concert for the proper objectives, they do not know what strategy to use. Proudhon thinks that this lack was demonstrated by their electoral behavior in 1863-1864. The proletariat's "debut was at once a great victory and a great mistake,"[41] for, though it co-operated to affirm mutualist principles, it did not act prudently. By participating in the elections and by proposing worker candidates, it helped shore up a system that could only damage its own true interests.

How, then, does Proudhon suggest that the workers lead the peasants and middle class to victory? He does not offer any clear advice. True, he warns the workers that they must find points of common interest with the peasants. Nothing is more important than that these two great classes agree on the measures to be pursued in common.[42] It is also true that Proudhon tells the proletariat and its allies to follow a tactic of withdrawal. "Since the old world rejects us," there is nothing to do but "separate ourselves from it radically."[43] What this involves is not very clearly stated, although Proudhon is sure that "it is the most powerful weapon, as it is the most loyal," i.e., that it is both effective and respectful.[44] Certainly it in-

---

[40] *Ibid.*, p. 92.            [41] *Ibid.*, p. 73.

[42] *Ibid.*, p. 70. As for the commercial middle class, it "will soon be only too happy to obtain" an alliance with the workers, whatever terms are offered, p. 231.

[43] *Ibid.*, p. 236.            [44] *Ibid.*, p. 237.

cludes avoidance of all involvement in the established political system. It may also entail, as the syndicalists later believed, the founding of embryonic mutualist institutions, open to all partisans of the cause. We will never know exactly what, if anything, Proudhon had in mind when he outlined his tactic of withdrawal, because he died before he could say.[45]

Unfortunately, nothing he might have said could have protected his final strategy from ineffectiveness. His strict adherence to the rules of respect led him to favor an excessively mild version of withdrawal, just as it had earlier led him to support excessively mild sorts of education and economic reform. That withdrawal is a respectful tactic is easily seen. By retiring from established institutions the workers would in no way hinder the conduct and choice of others; they would simply have as little to do with them as possible.

Proudhon also thought withdrawal was effective. He believed that if the workers and their allies retreated from the established order, they would develop their self-reliance and swell their ranks until they became a self-conscious majority of the population. Presumably, he believed that experience with embryonic mutualism would convince participants of its advantages and win new partisans. It can at least be said of this belief that it is better warranted than his earlier ones, since there is more

---

[45] It may be precisely because it was so inexplicit that this part of his theory had some influence. Many non-Marxist members of the First International, as well as later syndicalists, said they were indebted to Proudhon for his strategy of withdrawal.

reason to think that practicing mutualists will develop enthusiasm for the cause than that education or free credit will have this result. Hence, the tactic of withdrawal comes closer than any other to meeting Proudhon's strategic needs.

But even withdrawal does not meet them. The most it could produce would be a mutualist majority. The problem remains of dealing with the minority who choose to stay outside the camp. Proudhon offers different solutions to this problem. On occasion he urges persuasion of the abstainers in a way that respects their aims and conduct. "After having made known their idea," by developing it in isolation, "the working classes . . . convert all of France to it."[46] Here mutualism is established by "the reflective will of all," without infringing on any dissenter's freedom.[47] Unfortunately, reliance on this ill-defined process of conversion is a prescription for failure. The mutualists, even though a majority, would tie their hands by such strict adherence to their own principles.[48] For this reason, even Proudhon's most promising tactic does not fill his strategic needs. At the end of his quest, as at the beginning, his perfectionist determination to use respectful means led him to choose an ineffective strategy.

[46] *Ibid.*, p. 74.    [47] *Conf.*, p. 174.

[48] At some points in the *Capacité*, Proudhon seems to realize this. He then suggests that the mutualist majority use force against dissenters, rather than persuasion, pp. 101, 240. This version of the tactic of withdrawal is certainly more vigorous than the other, but it is just as inadequate. For it too assumes (mistakenly) that withdrawal can win a majority of the population to the mutualist cause.

## Misdirected Expediency: Proudhon as a Collaborator

Was this choice necessary? In other words, could Proudhon have decided on a more vigorous strategy without betraying his basic values? There can be no doubt that such a choice would have entailed sacrifice of perfection. Whatever the outcome, decisive tactics would have been tainted with coercion and so could not have conformed perfectly with the imperatives of respect. But a sacrifice of perfection is not the same as a betrayal of the rules of respect. If imperfect means could have begotten mutualism, they would have been more faithful to the ideal of respect than pure means, which did not. The central issue, therefore, is whether Proudhon would have remained truer to his principles by abandoning perfection than he did by adhering to it.

Fortunately, this matter need not be decided wholly in the abstract. At one critical point in his life, after Louis Napoleon's *coup d'état*, Proudhon gave up perfection by resorting to tactics that were vigorous, and hence inherently disrespectful. If this anomalous strategy could have created a respectful world, then his habitual reliance on a pure strategy was unnecessary. By consistently favoring this more vigorous course he could have moved society down the road to mutualism.

As late as the summer of 1851 Proudhon was still hoping that his doctrine would more or less spontaneously "seize hold of the masses and propel them into the future with irresistible impetus."[49] The coup dashed these hopes. The masses had proved by their inertness that they were

[49] *I.G.*, p. 121.

indifferent to liberation. By their indecision, the leftist parliamentary leaders had shown that they were inept and unreliable. Counter-revolutionary forces now occupied all the seats of power and could not be expected to relinquish them. Faced by this situation, Proudhon had to reassess the prospects for attaining mutualism with respect. Formerly he had believed that the worst consequence of rigorous adherence to his principles was indefinite postponement of success. As he then assessed matters, hostile forces were not strong enough to increase oppression; the most they could do was maintain the status quo. Now that Bonaparte was in power, reliance on morally pure tactics entailed more than postponement of success: it invited defeat. Since the new regime would certainly intensify oppression, refusal to interfere with aims or actions would now mean suicide for the mutualist cause. In the face of a militant and powerful opposition, the mutualists would have to be militant too, even if this meant violating their principles.

The first sign that Proudhon was abandoning perfection appears in a note of March 1852. Whereas formerly he had judged tactics "strictly from the viewpoint of principles," now he complains that "we democrats and socialists always start from moral principles, and that is why we lose all our contests."[50] Proudhon had learned his lesson. However moral the rules of respect might be, their application to tactics was highly inexpedient. Immediately after drawing this lesson, he began work on a strategy intended to succeed at any price. The outcome of this

[50] Cited in Dolléans, p. 252.

effort was *La révolution sociale démontrée par le coup d'état du deux décembre*, the book in which, by reasoning "like Themistocles or Machiavelli, from the viewpoint of expediency," he defended collaboration with Bonaparte.[51]

This strategy would have accorded with Proudhon's principles only if it would really have led to mutualist reform. On its face, collaboration with a usurping dictator hardly seems likely to have done so. It is therefore not surprising that Proudhon's espousal of collaboration has become a focus of controversy. Some of his severest critics have ascribed his strategy in the *Révolution sociale* to defection from the cause of freedom.[52] Others have traced it to admiration for Bonaparte.[53] About the most that sympathetic writers have been able to do is point out that his collaborationism is no more than a momentary aberration.[54]

The truth is that Proudhon's personal *justification* of collaboration is perfectly consistent with his highest values. What conflicts with them is its *expectable results*.

[51] *R.S.*, p. 157.

[52] See, e.g., Georges Cogniot, *Proudhon et la démagogie bonapartiste* (Paris, 1958), p. 27.

[53] Among those taking this line are Karl Heinz Bremer, "Der sozialistische Kaiser," *Die Tat*, xxx (1938), p. 160. Bremer's motive for adopting this view is obvious. He wants to enroll Proudhon in the ranks of Bonaparte's admirers. More recently, George Lichtheim has taken a similar position, for less obvious reasons. See *The Concept of Ideology*, Vintage Book edition (New York, 1967), p. 260.

[54] E.g., Georges Guy-Grand, *Pour connaître la pensée de Proudhon* (Paris, 1947), p. 82. Some friends of Proudhon simply ignore the whole problem, e.g., George Woodcock, *Pierre-Joseph Proudhon* (New York, 1956), pp. 178, 182.

It is this gap between Proudhon's subjective reasons for favoring collaboration, on the one hand, and its objective consequences, on the other, that explain the controversy it has provoked. Those who think he remained true to the cause of freedom stress his personal grounds for favoring collaboration; his critics point to its likely consequences.

Proudhon had two explicit reasons for backing collaboration. The first was a conviction that the Republicans' failure to collaborate with Bonaparte had caused their defeat in the period just before the *coup d'état*. He was especially critical of their attack on Bonaparte in November 1851, just after they had finished supporting his unsuccessful campaign to restore universal suffrage. This attack arose from the Republicans' fear of a coup, and from their wish to disassociate themselves. Proudhon accuses them of a grave blunder here. Everyone knew the coup was coming; by protesting in advance, the Republicans may have saved their principles, but they lost their power. "Instead of mounting a purely personal attack on Louis Bonaparte, [the Republicans] had only to keep quiet and prepare to divide the fruits of victory with him. Would it not have been better ... for Michel (de Bourges) to have been minister of State or president of the Council on December 4, than for him to have fled to an inglorious exile in Brussels?"[55] The effective course for the Republicans, Proudhon is saying, was to collaborate with the new regime and influence it from within, rather than to oppose it from without.

[55] *R.S.*, p. 157.

Proudhon's other reason for backing collaboration was his firm belief that the new government would advance the mutualist cause, if only it received the proper guidance. He feared that if this "power, still without roots, just as surprised as the nation at its existence," were left to its own devices, "the revolution would retrogress by ten degrees."[56] This disaster could be avoided. If Proudhon and his sympathizers rallied to the regime and offered it their guidance, it was sure to be followed. "The Second of December is the signal for a forward march on the revolutionary road, and . . . Louis Napoleon is its general," whether or not he knows it. The mutualists' job is to inform him of his role; then he is sure to fulfill it.[57]

Despite his faith in collaboration, Proudhon had an inkling of its dangers, for he decided to espouse it with reluctance, and tried to put conditions on it that would forestall unfavorable results. His *Carnets* disclose that his decision to write the *Révolution sociale* caused him great anguish. After working on it for only about a week, he had a change of heart. "I am giving it up. It seems to me that I am deceiving myself about the utility of this pamphlet. The more I think about it and the more I write, the more I seem to see that there is only one rational way to deal with the reigning order of things, that is with total war and by sounding the alarm against it as against a

---

[56] *Ibid.*, p. 113.

[57] *Ibid.*, p. 177. Whether or not Proudhon thought Bonaparte was aware of his "destiny" is a subject of dispute. Cogniot, p. 29, says he did think so, but cf. *R.S.*, p. 295.

gang of robbers."[58] At this point, the vanity of collaboration seems to have dawned on him. He questions its utility, thus betraying doubts about its favorable consequences. But the counsel of all-out war suggested here is really no more likely to succeed than collaboration. Proudhon never seriously considered any other strategies.

Hence, it is not surprising to find him writing in his notebook six days later, after a long meditative walk, "I have returned home with the intention to publish something after all." In the same entry he lists some objections to this course: "I understand that this work can only compromise me seriously without compensating advantages. It involves participating in the crime to a certain extent, by breathing some life into it. . . . To find a way out of a nest of thieves, an explanation for an ambush! a meaning for perjury! an excuse for cowardice, a point to imbecility! a rationale and a cause for tyranny! To do this is to prostitute reason, it is to abuse one's powers to think, observe and judge."[59] These objections, unlike his earlier ones, are based on grounds of principle. Collaboration is condemned as intrinsically evil, whatever its result, not as imprudent owing to undesired consequences. Arguments such as these could not be decisive, given Proudhon's disenchantment with perfectionism. Hence, the *Révolution sociale* was published three months later, despite its author's serious reservations.

[58] *Carnet* entry of April 7, 1852, cited in Edouard Dolléans and Georges Duveau, "Introduction" to *R.S.*, p. 70.

[59] *Carnet* entry of April 13, 1852, cited in *ibid.*, p. 71, ellipsis in original.

Scrutiny of this book shows that Proudhon's qualms were not confined to his preliminary jottings. In the published text he went out of his way to prevent unfavorable consequences from collaboration by strictly limiting the conditions under which it could occur. Hence, despite the caricatures, Proudhon was no sycophantic admirer of the Prince President, willing to go to any lengths to curry favor. On the contrary, the dictator would have to go extraordinarily far in Proudhon's direction to enlist his support. He would have to reform the constitution by making it more democratic. "The President's powers are out of all proportion to his duties: it is no longer an idea that reigns, but a man."[60] Nor is this all. Since "industrial liberty is inseparable from political liberty," Bonaparte would have to carry out social and economic, as well as political, reform.[61] In short, he would have to begin building mutualism, and by respectful means. "The government . . . is caught between anarchy and arbitrary rule."[62] Unless it chooses the former, and works for it by example and education, mutualist collaboration is to be denied it.

These stipulations certainly qualify the collaboration espoused in the *Révolution sociale*, but they do not eliminate it. No doubt the book, strictly interpreted, does rule out collaboration. So exacting are the conditions set for collaboration that they could not possibly be met. Such a strict interpretation is too subtle, however, because it overlooks the book's impact on its audience. The rather casuistic argument of the *Révolution sociale* was sure to go

[60] *R.S.*, p. 218.   [61] *Ibid.*, p. 275.   [62] *Ibid.*, p. 276.

over the public's head; all it would grasp was that Proudhon, an apostle of liberty, had lent the dictator his good name and support. Hence the book was bound to strengthen the new regime, rather than the cause of freedom, whatever its author's intention.[63]

This conclusion helps resolve the central question about Proudhon's tactics—whether he could have remained truer to his principles by abandoning perfection or by adhering to it. On the one occasion when he sacrificed perfection in order to recommend vigorous tactics, the measures he favored did not lead to the end sought. A misdirected though vigorous strategy like collaboration is even less compatible with his ideals than the impotent ones he usually favored. The latter could not build mutualism, but at least they conformed to the imperatives of respect. Collaboration, though equally ineffective, lacked this compensating virtue. Being incompatible with the norms of respect as well as unable to realize them, it was the worst possible tactic for the partisans of mutualism.

### Radicalism, Perfection, and Tactical Effectiveness

Though Proudhon failed to discover an effective but imperfect strategy, it is far from certain that none could possibly have been devised. Such an inference could be drawn only if Proudhon had been a capable tactician;

[63] That the book would harm the cause of freedom, whatever its intention, was noted at the time by Léon Plée. "Must M. Proudhon furnish arms to the reactionaries and strengthen our enemies whenever he speaks?" Article from *Le siècle* (August 19, 1852), reprinted in *R.S.*, p. 370.

otherwise, the possibility would remain that a shrewder strategist could have found a path to mutualism.

There can be no doubt that Proudhon was a singularly inept tactician. The clearest sign of this is his expectation of mutualist reform by Bonaparte, an expectation which bespeaks a total misreading of Bonaparte's character, an erroneous assessment of his intentions, and a grave misjudgment of the risks in supporting him, with however many qualifications. To be sure, Proudhon, who thought Bonaparte a "génie médiocre" was not the only one to misread his character. Thiers' famous boutade, "c'est un crétin que l'on mènera," shows that he was of the same opinion. But Thiers was wise enough to avoid the conclusion that collaboration was the best policy. It is also true that in early 1852 the Prince President had not yet made his intentions crystal clear. Proudhon was not the only one to be duped by Bonaparte's professions of concern for the poor and his re-establishment of universal suffrage into thinking (or hoping) that he represented a victory for the left against a threatening monarchist restoration. The fact remains that no one else on the left was reckless enough to preach collaboration with the new regime. Had Proudhon been more astute, he too would have seen the dangers in such a course.

Perhaps the failure of Proudhon's strategic vision can be ascribed to his perfectionist bent of mind. To think strategically means to use prudence, by compromising values in the light of probabilities. This is just the sort of activity in which anyone like Proudhon, who finds moral compromise outrageous, is bound to be inept.

Whatever its explanation, Proudhon's ineptness at strategy means that his failure to discover a tactic for begetting mutualism is no proof of such a tactic's unavailability. An argument to prove this must show that even if Proudhon had been a master of strategic prudence, he still could not have found a way to mutualist reform.

Whether or not prudence can promise success for a political change depends on the scope and clarity of the goals being sought. If they are modest, clearly defined, and attainable in the short run, prudence can show how to reach them. But if they are comprehensive, vaguely conceived, and attainable only in the distant future, prudence cannot be of any help. In such cases the choice of means will always be treacherous and unreliable. To reach a vast and vague end, extremely energetic and wide-ranging measures are required. Such measures are sure to have numerous unexpected consequences, and may have none of the intended ones. Hence the goal sought will not be reached or, if it is, unwanted side effects will be produced.[64] The conclusion is obvious. Since it is just this sort of imprecise but all-inclusive goal that Proudhon aspired for, even the most skillful use of prudence could not have helped him. Prudence promises no greater chance of success than the perfectionism that claimed his allegiance.

It can even be argued that Proudhon's adherence to perfectionism was fortunate, since it kept him from taking steps calculated to reach his goals but actually leading to disaster. Had he been indifferent to applying the im-

---

[64] See the judicious elaboration of this point by George Kateb in *Utopia and its Enemies* (N.Y., 1963), pp. 44-67.

peratives of respect to tactics, his radical objectives and keen sense of the obstacles to reaching them might well have induced him to favor treacherous strategies. The moral element in his thought prevented this, by counteracting the dangerous alliance of radicalism and realism formed by its other two ingredients.

Since prudence is no better than perfection in finding a way to mutualism, it appears that Proudhon's strategic problem is insoluble. Before this conclusion can be drawn, a third way of devising tactics must be considered. Perhaps a method that used both principled *and* prudential reasoning could satisfy Proudhon's strategic needs. Such a method would involve a constant readaption of ends to the changing conditions that affect their attainability, and a repeated testing of means to assure their accordance with the values being sought. Certainly this is how tactics must be arrived at if ends are not to become "disembodied rituals" and means are not to "contradict the values originally stated." The ethical consequences of decisions about means and the practical consequences of decisions about ends must receive equal consideration.[65]

Unfortunately, this procedure is not open to Proudhon. It is a suitable method only for a theorist who does not favor wholesale change and so is willing to trim his aspirations when they are difficult to realize. This Proudhon was not prepared to do. Respect is a value so supremely im-

[65] See Gunnar Myrdal, *Value in Social Theory* (London, 1958), pp. 157-64, 210-13; and Stanley Hoffmann, ed. *Contemporary Theory in International Relations* (Englewood Cliffs, 1960), pp. 187-89. The phrases quoted in the preceding sentence are from the latter source.

portant that its embodiment in ends can no more be compromised than its application to means. Since he was committed to the integral attainment of respect and faced a world where such attainment was extremely difficult, Proudhon was left with only the two equally cruel alternatives this chapter has described. No matter how great his strategic talents, he would have had to choose between relying on ineffective though vigorous tactics and accepting some form of perfectionist "attente révolutionnaire." His radicalism left him no third choice. Given his premises, and existing conditions, his problem was both unavoidable and insoluble.

If there is anything inexplicable about Proudhon's attitude toward tactics it is not that he shifted between policies of misdirected opportunism and impotent perfectionism, but that he so rarely chose the first and so doggedly stuck to the second. Adherence to morally pure strategies ruled out all chance of foreseeable success, yet he remained true to them, only once succumbing to expediency and, even more striking, never to complacency or despair. Nothing would have been easier than to use the manifest obstacles to the achievement of mutualism as an excuse for indolence, for refraining from efforts to improve society while yet professing to favor radical change. Here, as at so many other points in his political theorizing, Proudhon shows that blend of sincerity and single-mindedness in the face of overpowering adversity which is his signal intellectual trait.

Proudhon's tactical stance, and its dilemma, anticipate those of contemporary libertarian radicals. Like him, they are uncompromising advocates of radical change. Like him, they are unwilling to use coercive means to achieve it. A final resemblance is that they too recognize that few approve of their ends and that even fewer are willing to help achieve them.[66] Their position differs from Proudhon's in that they rarely wish to change society as profoundly as he did. This makes their tactical problem somewhat easier. But their situation differs from his in another way that offsets this advantage. Whether in Europe or America, they are faced by an affluent, self-satisfied society, far less incipiently revolutionary than the industrializing France to which Proudhon addressed himself. Hence, though they want less than he did, their chances of getting it by morally pure means are also smaller. Given existing conditions and the radicalism of their principles, they, like him, must choose between a course of expedient compromise that violates their principles and one of moral purity that condemns them to impotence. If they take the second alternative, their only remaining choice, like that of their predecessor, is between using perfectionism as an excuse for inaction or as a support for perservering without hope of foreseeable success.

[66] Herbert Marcuse, in *One Dimensional Man* (London, 1964), takes all three of these positions: (1) "Society is irrational as a whole," p. ix. (2) "The slaves must be *free for* their liberation before they can become free. . . . The end must be operative in the means to attain it," p. 41. (3) "The vast majority accepts, and is made to accept this [irrational] society," p. xiii.

# CHAPTER VII

## Explanation and Criticism

NOT even the most understanding student of Proudhon's thought is likely to spare it of all criticism. Its onesided view of human nature, its biased slant on history, its self-defeating moral rigor, its sweeping denunciation of the status quo, not to mention its extravagant mutualist outcome—all these features provide inviting targets for attack. Yet not all of them may be fairly criticized. Some parts of Proudhon's theory, like its moral rigor, follow from premises which, being judgments of intrinsic value, are beyond reproach. Others, like its radical critique and its proposal for mutualist reform, are undeserving of criticism because they were forced on Proudhon by circumstances he could not control. Analysis of these circumstances should therefore help to account for his most implausible ideas.

### French Authority and Proudhonian Implausibility

One circumstance that drove Proudhon toward radical criticism and sweeping reform was the pattern of authority prevalent in France. Alexis de Tocqueville was the first to describe this pattern and to trace its political consequences. Authority in France, he said, consisted of a "single central power controlling public administration throughout the country" by means of "rigid rules" covering "every detail of administration."[1] The consequences of this pattern of authority, according to Tocqueville, were political apathy and the division of society into isolated compartments. The monarchy segregated social classes in order to govern more effectively. Being segregated, they became ever more politically indifferent and incapable.[2]

Recently Michel Crozier has applied Tocqueville's analysis to contemporary France. He sees the same kind of authority still producing the same effects. Today "the impersonality of rules" and "the centralization of decisions" cause "strata isolation" and "apathy in public affairs" just as they did under the old regime.[3] But Crozier also sees something else, that escaped Tocqueville. He finds that Frenchmen use the pattern of authority they encounter in political life to govern their social lives as well. They relate to others through the medium of impersonal rules, and then unyieldingly stand up for their rights. Conversely, they avoid direct dealing as much as possible. "To compromise, to make deals, to adjust to other people's claims is frowned upon; it is considered better to restrict oneself and to remain free within the narrow limits one has fixed or even those one has had to accept."[4] Social relations thus reinforce the very pattern of political authority that created them in the first place. To sum up, authority in France, as described by both Crozier and Tocqueville, takes the form of an aloof lawgiver, who imposes fair but

[1] Alexis de Tocqueville, *The Old Regime and the French Revolution*, Anchor Book edition (New York, 1955), pp. 57, 67.

[2] *Ibid.*, p. 107.

[3] Michel Crozier, *The Bureaucratic Phenomenon* (Chicago, 1964), pp. 213, 220.

[4] *Ibid.*, p. 223.

unilateral decisions on all members of society. The main product of this pattern of authority is a disposition to obey and exploit impartial rules. Its main ban is on compromise and bargaining.

The bearing of this pattern of authority on Proudhon's attitude toward it is easily seen. Once he had decided that authority in France, far from being advantageous, was nothing but a prejudice, he had to condemn it radically and work for its total abolition. No attempt at moderating it could possibly succeed, since habits of submission to it were too deeply entrenched. Nor was this all. Since submission to monocratic legal authority and distaste for bargaining were mutually reinforcing, a successful attack on the first called for rehabilitation of the second. Proudhon's whole reformative enterprise, being meant to take place in France, had to glorify bargaining; otherwise it could not possibly reach its intended goal.

Tocqueville too sought to undermine the traditional French pattern of authority, and for much the same reason as Proudhon. Both writers attacked it as destructive of liberty. But whereas Proudhon envisaged a totally new form of social order, Tocqueville, who favored an aristocratic ideal of freedom, proposed to rebuild a feudal structure, to the greatest extent possible.[5] This restoration involved a revival of religion as a weapon against state control and a reordering of government to strengthen local units and voluntary associations. The second of these planks is reminiscent of Proudhon's federalism, but the

[5] For an excellent analysis of Tocqueville's aristocratic view of freedom see Raymond Aron, *Essai sur les libertés* (Paris, 1965), pp. 24-27.

resemblance is only formal. The aim of Tocqueville's decentralization was to create a new aristocracy under modern democratic circumstances. He wanted local and associational units to "take the place of the individual authority of the nobles."[6] Proudhon's federalism, on the other hand, was to be a substitute for both centralized *and* feudal authority. Hence it is not surprising that he harshly criticized Tocqueville. "Why, in his book on *L'Ancien régime ou la Révolution* [sic], does M. de Tocqueville join the ranks of those extolling an alliance of aristocracy and democracy, of Catholicism and liberty? The reason is that M. de Tocqueville, who like M. Guizot is an excellent Christian, is a perfect non-believer on matters of liberty and equality."[7] In Proudhon's opinion, Tocqueville does not effectively combat French legalism and centralization. He merely restores an old pattern of authority that is even more objectionable.

Although the pattern of French authority goes far toward explaining the vehemence of Proudhon's critique and the oddness of his proposal for reform, it does not markedly help to explain his doubts about the viability of his proposal. Why did he worry so much that his scheme for bargaining would lead to war?

The theorist in the history of political thought whose proposals most resemble Proudhon's did not have this fear. This theorist was G.D.H. Cole, in his Guild Socialist phase. Cole went almost as far as Proudhon toward dismantling government. Like Proudhon, he suggested that

[6] Alexis de Tocqueville, *Democracy in America*, ed. Phillips Bradley (New York, 1945), i, 9.

[7] *Justice*, iii, 239.

legal and political regulation be replaced by compromise among interested parties themselves. But in Cole's vision the dangers of bargaining do not figure at all. Negotiation between the Guilds is obviously important, yet no effort is made to define the conditions under which it is to take place. Bargaining is casually mentioned; Cole simply takes it for granted that this is the practice by which disputes will be settled.[8] Cole's sanguine attitude toward bargaining is best explained as a symptom of his optimism about social harmony. "The essence of the whole proposal," he explains, "is that the producers should be put 'on their honor' to do their best."[9] Cole implicitly assumes that society can handle its affairs in harmony without coercion. Assuming this, he need not worry about the problem of safety.

This assumption may hold true in England; it certainly does not in France, for there pluralism does not lead to harmony. Tocqueville was not the last to lament that French attempts to decentralize, even though half-hearted, have had disastrous results.[10] The very pattern of authority that pluralism is supposed to change makes its adoption dangerous, by disposing people to stand up unyieldingly for their rights. Deep ideological cleavages add to the dangers of pluralism by fostering intransigence between potential negotiators. Since the sense of fair play in

[8] G.D.H. Cole, *Guild Socialism Restated* (London, 1920), pp. 68, 147.

[9] *Ibid.*, p. 88.

[10] Tocqueville, *Old Regime*, p. 196; Stanley Hoffmann, "The Areal Division of Powers in the Writings of French Political Thinkers," in *Area and Power*, ed. Arthur Maass (Glencoe, 1959), pp. 128-29.

France is simply not vivid enough to warrant putting contenders "on their honor," Proudhon, unlike Cole, could not take the harmonious operation of bargaining for granted. French contenders are roguish swindlers, not honest gentlemen. They may be transformed into proud duelists, but never into genteel cricketeers; even this transformation will be difficult.[11] Proudhon's determination to tame contenders who are not disposed to bargain peacefully accounts for his obsession with war and his resort to ever harsher measures to prevent it.

While conditions in France are responsible for some of the quirks in Proudhon's thought, they cannot be blamed for all of them. Given Proudhon's values and the world he faced, he had no choice but to aim at replacing established authority with bargaining. But this is not to say that his implausibilities are entirely justified, or even excused, by circumstances. The truth is that neither Proudhon's values nor environmental conditions forced him to reach the conclusions analyzed in this study. Both allowed generous scope for a different, and more acceptable, position. His failure to reach one is due to faulty theorizing, not to uncontrollable circumstances. There is ample warrant for asking exactly what is wrong with his theory and how it may be improved.

### Respect or Autonomy?

Proudhon's political thought is above all else a liberating endeavor. It is an attempt to discover how we must change the world in order to be free. Viewed from this

---

[11] Proudhon was far from hostile to duels and fought one himself, *G.P.*, pp. 219-20.

angle, its strongest point is its concept of a totally free man, autonomous in the sense that he not only acts as he pleases but decides as he pleases too. Most political writers deny that a man must enjoy liberty of choice in order to be free. If nothing prevents me from executing my decision, they say, then I qualify as free in the full sense of that word. What this thesis overlooks is that the decision I am free to carry out may itself be made without freedom. My choice may be impeded by a wide variety of restraints, such as overwhelming desire, ignorance, and social pressure. In such cases I would be deemed free according to the usual concept of liberty, but not according to Proudhon's more discerning one.[12]

Despite his discernment in making autonomy the goal of reform, Proudhon went only a short way toward showing how to reach it. The main reason he was unable to go further is that, rather than aiming directly for autonomy, he tried to achieve respect instead. Both goals have the same liberating effect on action, since both call for release from impediments to conduct. But they differ in their effect on choice in a way that makes respect far less suitable than autonomy as the aim of libertarian reform. Respect, unlike autonomy, imposes a duty to identify with the choices of others. The unfortunate effect of this duty is to curtail the very freedom of decision that Proudhon was anxious to defend. In most cases, to be sure, the duty of others to identify with my choices protects my freedom

---

[12] For a convincing argument that free decision is as vital for political liberty as is free action see John L. Mothershead, Jr., "Some Reflections on the Meaning of Freedom," *Journal of Philosophy*, XLIX, No. 21 (1952), pp. 667-72.

of decision. Persons who identify with my choices obviously will not interfere with them. But in one crucial situation this duty sharply curtails my freedom to decide as I please: when I encounter a person who chooses to do something I dislike. My duty to identify with his choice then restricts my own freedom of decision, by binding me to identify with a choice I would prefer to oppose. In short, Proudhonian respect obliges sacrifice of free decision for the sake of the wishes of other persons.

This shortcoming in the norm of respect shows that there is no place for it in a theory aimed at achieving autonomy by securing not only free action, but free decision as well. Fortunately, it can be easily dispensed with, because it is surely a mistake to think that a man's freedom of choice depends on others' identifying with his decisions. It may be pleasant to enjoy such identification, but it is a quite unnecessary condition of free choice. To decide freely, I must be exempt from restraint upon my will. All that is needed to assure this is that others refrain from *interfering* with my decisions; they need not *respect* them.[13]

Hence the basic correction to Proudhon's theory needed to make possible the freedom he seeks to achieve is the substitution of *autonomy* for respect as the goal of libertarian reform. The proper aim of liberating endeavor is

[13] From a philosophical point of view, much more might be deemed necessary for free decision than mere absence of interference by others. But all parties to the philosophical controversy about free will would admit that the absence of such interference is a necessary condition for free decision, whatever else may be required.

not free action mixed with unfree choice, as it was for Proudhon, but action and choice that are equally free.

## A Test for Autonomous Choice

Proudhon's mistaken definition of his goal set him off on the wrong track. He would have been less likely to reach the wrong destination if he had realized that social pressure blocks free choice. Had he seen this, he could not have said that people bound by the force of public opinion could still be free. If libertarian reform is not to repeat this mistake, a test must be added to its theory for distinguishing genuinely autonomous choice from choice made under the influence of social pressure.

The simplest test is the one first used by the romantics. Most of them thought society "a foreign body which the individual simply 'finds' there confronting him against his will."[14] Having postulated a watertight separation between man and society, it was easy for them to distinguish self-directed from conformist choice. I choose autonomously when I follow the guidance of self-produced norms. I am a conformist when I follow the norms that society prescribes to me from outside. The romantic criterion looks solely to the origin of the norms or directives on which decision turns. Self-direction involves adherence to internally produced norms of choice, conformity to those which are externally imposed.

This test may be simple, but it is certainly inadequate, because it overlooks the fact that only a very small number of the norms used to guide decision have a purely per-

[14] Judith Shklar, *After Utopia* (Princeton, 1957), pp. 132-33.

sonal origin. Almost all of them are absorbed from out-side.[15] To follow the romantics by using exemption from social influence as the sign of autonomy thus guarantees in advance that virtually no cases of autonomous choice will ever be found.

Some of the existentialists, our contemporary romantics, draw a line between autonomy and conformity that takes more account of society's influence on the will. They admit that public opinion may be internalized and hence that society is not, strictly speaking, a "foreign body," controlling solely by sanction and reward. But they immediately add that the volitional directives absorbed by an individual from his society are not the only kind he has; there are others immanent within him and authentically his own.[16] An autonomous man follows this second type of directive, a conformist follows the first. Because it acknowledges society's influence on the will, the existentialist test for autonomy is superior to the romantic one, superior, but still not satisfactory, since it too ascribes existence to a core of self-produced, socially unmodified norms of choice. This ascription makes the existentialists' test just as pointless as that of the romantics. Since there are hardly any self-produced norms of choice, one can find almost no cases of autonomy, as existentially defined.

Both the romantics and the existentialists draw lines

[15] Only the tiny class of persons who qualify as moral innovators use norms of choice that are indisputably self-produced. The norms used by innovators must be self-produced since, being original, they cannot possibly be absorbed from outside.

[16] Edward A. Tiryakian, *Sociologism and Existentialism* (Englewood Cliffs, N.J., 1962), p. 152.

between autonomy and conformity that make the search for the former futile; they describe a more exalted kind of self-directed choice than social realities allow them to achieve. The sociologists, as if learning the lesson of the romantics' failure, propose to take the facts more seriously. Some, at least, think that the impact of society on the will makes it impossible to draw any line between autonomy and conformity. Conformity is the only reality. We may sometimes imagine that we are deciding according to self-produced directives, but what strike us as our own norms of choice are actually "forced upon us by the ways of the culture and the socialization process we undergo."[17] The thesis that men can choose according to self-produced norms is a naïve fiction. A person sometimes denies that his standards are absorbed from others, especially when he chooses to defy a prevalent convention, but he is mistaken. All that happens then, according to many sociologists, is that he follows a norm taken over from a deviant reference group. The important point is that he has nonetheless absorbed his standard from a social milieu, so that it cannot properly be called self-produced.

The bearing of the sociologists' attitude toward autonomy on the prospect for liberation is no different from that of the romantics. The romantics assure that the search for liberation will not reach its destination, the sociologists that it will never begin. Both, in their distinctive ways, condemn it to failure. For despite their differences, romantics and sociologists agree that men who absorb their

[17] David Riesman, *The Lonely Crowd*, Anchor Book edition (New York, 1953), p. 300.

norms of choice from outside cannot make autonomous decisions.

Fortunately, there is a way to escape this gloomy conclusion. Let us grant all the factual propositions made by the sociologists. We shall assume that they have forever refuted the claim, still made by the existentialists, that man can choose according to self-produced directives. Their thesis that norms of choice are always the products of social pressure will also be accepted. From these premises it follows incontestably that self-direction in the romantic sense of choice according to self-produced norms is an illusion. But this does not mean that no autonomy can be achieved at all. Even if all man's norms are absorbed from society, ample room for self-direction remains.

To think otherwise is to confuse autonomy with deviance; it is to commit the romantic fallacy of equating self-direction with total rejection of conventional norms. The romantics' abhorrence of social influence and their ardent thirst for spontaneity led to this error. We must be sober enough not to repeat it. The real sign of autonomy is not that a man rejects all prevalent norms of choice, but that his grounds for upholding the norms he accepts, be they prevalent or not, are of the proper kind. Description of these grounds will therefore open the door to liberation that the sociologists seem to have locked so securely.

Proudhon can be of help here, because he distinguishes correctly between autonomy and conformity in the political and religious spheres, if not the social one. In *Propriété* he maintained that autonomous choice does not call for rejecting all volitional directives whose origin is political. I can accept them while remaining my own master if I can support my acceptance with proof of their validity. If a man "no longer obeys because the king commands, but because the king convinces, it is clear that henceforth he recognizes no external authority and that he has become his own king."[18] In *Justice* Proudhon applies the same argument to man's relationship with God. A person subject to religious influence may qualify as autonomous without rejecting all divine imperatives. In fact, he "may bow down before the majesty of a Supreme Being, but only under the express condition that this being deigns to give him explanations."[19] The distinction Proudhon makes in the political and religious spheres also applies to society. I can accept socially prevalent norms of choice, while retaining my autonomy, provided I have proof of their validity.

The only way to secure this proof is through critical evaluation. Such evaluation has two forms.[20] Either I must appraise possible norms of choice according to a standard, or else I must test them by a method of verification. In either case, I base my acceptance of the norms I uphold on systematic proof of their validity. Acceptance backed by proof of this kind can be given to any norm, however conventional, without impairment of autonomy. Unless I go through the process of validating my norms by some standard or method that seems appropriate to me, I have no way of telling whether I have absorbed them unwittingly from my culture. Consequently, I have no assurance that my decisions are exempt from social pres-

[18] *Prop.*, p. 338.
[19] *Justice*, 1, 366.     [20] Mothershead, pp. 669-70.

sure. But if I am careful to accept only those norms which pass methodical tests of validity, then I can be sure that, no matter how conventional they may be, I uphold them because I think them valid, not because they are prevalent. In other words, the process of critical evaluation serves as a yardstick for judging convention, as a shield against indiscriminately accepting it and as a weapon for resisting it when it proves to be invalid.

Making dependence on self-validated norms the sign of autonomous choice reopens the door to liberation which is closed by the sociologists. If decisions, to count as autonomous, must depend on self-produced norms, then autonomy cannot be achieved, but if they need depend only on self-validated ones, autonomy becomes attainable. While it may well be impossible to use norms of choice that lack a social origin, it is certainly possible to use ones that have been systematically validated. Hence the proper goal of liberating endeavor is not to encourage denial of convention—as it was for the romantics—but to strengthen the capacity for judging it by critical and methodical tests.

There is one major objection to this goal. The critic impressed by sociology is sure to claim that our so-called autonomous man is no less dependent on his social environment than an other-directed one. It is easy to say that autonomy means choosing according to norms that have passed some explicit test. But how does the self-directed man arrive at this test? His social experience surely has some influence, perhaps a decisive one. If this is the case, is he really any more autonomous than the person who relies directly on convention when he makes a choice? The decisions of both, after all, are subject to the pressures of society.

This objection goes too far. It is true that social pressure cannot be entirely escaped—except, perhaps, by moral innovators, who may be ignored. But there are differences in the degree of its influence. Though enjoyment of autonomy, as defined here, does not guarantee complete immunity from social pressure, it does assure some exemption from its power. An autonomous man, armed with a set of self-validated norms of choice, need not invariably follow expectations. Instead, he may conform discriminately, by following only those expectations which accord with the norms he has critically accepted. Society still constrains the autonomous man, because it affects his tests for the norms he accepts. The point, however, is that the non-autonomous man, lacking any such test at all, is even more constrained by society, because society affects his norms directly rather than through the medium of his tests for them. In short, the autonomous person at least escapes direct social determination of his volitional standards, even though his tests for them are subject to such determination. This difference of degree may not be great, but it is perhaps the greatest possible; in any event it is sufficient to permit significant release from social pressure.

### Some Implications of Autonomy for Society and Government

If the value of such release be granted in spite of its limits, the question that arises is: How can it be attained? This question will be only partly answered here, with some remarks suggested by Proudhon's ideas.

Nothing Proudhon ever defended can contribute more to autonomous choice than his pluralism, his support for diversity of social groups. Diversity fosters autonomy by encouraging people to examine their norms of choice critically. In a uniform society, men seldom think critically about the norms they use for making decisions, because everyone else uses them. In a diverse society, where different norms are accepted by different groups, critical examination is more widespread. Then, the availability of a variety of norms encourages each individual to question the validity of those he happens to uphold.

Although social diversity has great liberating power, Proudhon fails to make full use of it. He refuses to espouse the kind of thoroughgoing pluralism that would go furthest toward releasing choice from social restraint. What kept Proudhon from pressing for more diversity was the end he sought through use of a moderate amount. As we saw in an earlier chapter, he used diversity as a means to safeguard peace in his ideal society, by encouraging mutualist contenders to bargain rather than fight. The thoroughgoing pluralism that is most conducive to autonomy would defeat the objective of safeguarding peace, for it would incline mutualist contenders to question, and even reject, the principles on which mutualism depends.

The lesson of Proudhon's failure to make the most of pluralism's liberating power is easily drawn. Unless some method other than his is used to safeguard peace, the full benefits of diversity for autonomous choice cannot possibly be achieved. The most obvious alternative is legislation, the very device denounced by Proudhon as inconsistent with man's freedom. Fortunately, it can be shown that he was wrong to object to law on libertarian grounds.

Proudhon supports his libertarian objection to law by charging it with hindering action. Though this charge is true, it does not prove that law is always inimical to freedom. While all laws block free action to some extent, they need not reduce it on the whole. In fact, they may produce a net increase in options of conduct, even while eliminating some, by hindering more hindrances than they impose.

Suppose, nonetheless, for the sake of argument, that Proudhon is right to denounce law on libertarian grounds. Even if it is as coercive as he believes, law cannot be unequivocally condemned until its alternatives have been evaluated. The alternates may prove to be still more coercive.

One promising alternative to law as a safeguard for peace is the social pressure on which Proudhon himself relies. It is far from obvious, however, that social pressure is less coercive than law. Consider first whether social pressure impinges less than law on freedom to act as one pleases. The distinction between the absolute and the arbitrary is pertinent. Social pressure controls behavior less absolutely than law, because it is less severely sanctioned. Its penalties are milder than legal penalties, but, though social pressure controls behavior less absolutely than law, it also controls behavior more arbitrarily because its sanctions are more capricious. The penalties that sanction a law are limited by the terms of its enactment. Those that sanction a custom are limited only by the discretion of its enforcers. Hence persons subject to custom may not endure harsh penalties, but they are never safe from the comparatively mild penalties it does inflict.

Perhaps the nature of the sanctions of social and legal control make them equally inimical to free action, albeit for different reasons. In that case, the control that impinges least on free choice must be accounted superior from a libertarian point of view. There can be no doubt that law interferes less with decisions than social pressure. Legal control, applying to outward action, has little leverage on choice. Social pressure, through the process of internalization, wins direct access to those internal states of mind on which decision turns. Hence, even if law restricts action as much as custom does, it restricts choice so much less that it must be regarded by libertarians as the more suitable method for safeguarding peace.

Proudhon's evaluation of law is deficient not just because it misses the superiority of legislation to social pressure as a manager of conflict, but also because it fails to appreciate law's liberating power. It is true that in *Du principe fédératif* Proudhon finally made mutualism dependent on law. But even then, he viewed legislation as a necessary evil, rather than as a practice for advancing the mutualist cause. Whatever the contribution of law to mutualism may be, it can certainly help protect decisions from the constraint of society. Law has the same sort of liberating power as social pluralism, because it too can encourage people to think critically about their norms of choice.

Even if my society is pluralistically arranged, so that a diversity of norms prevail, I may still not critically examine those I accept. I may be unacquainted with the available alternatives. I may fear the social sanctions I would incur, even in a pluralistic environment, by questioning the norms prevalent in my immediate milieu. While social mobility can do something to counteract this situation, law can do more. It can protect persons disposed to question prevailing social norms by regulating the methods through which convention is enforced. Used in this way, law offers valuable support to freedom of decision, by guaranteeing the individual a kind of immunity from social pressure that he could not otherwise enjoy.

Once it is recognized that law has a creative role to play in the quest for liberation, a path to that end different from Proudhon's comes into sight. While never forgetting the point he emphasized, that, as Bentham also saw, "every law is an infraction of liberty,"[21] we must also remember that legal regulation may protect freedom, provided it is properly applied. Defense of autonomy calls, not for abolishing law or even minimizing its impact, but for calculating the benefits and costs to freedom of using it in alternative ways. For the execution of this calculus Proudhon's insights are of value, but they are insufficient. His political vision was telescopic. It penetrated into remote areas that others could not see, but the price of this magnification was a narrowed field of view. Many commonplaces that were apparent to others were invisible to him. Proudhon's telescopic vision explains his theory's weakness and its strength; it also has guided this critique

[21] Quoted in Isaiah Berlin, *Two Concepts of Liberty* (Oxford, 1958), p. 33.

of his position, which has tried to fill in a few of its blind spots without ignoring its perceptivity.

## Is Autonomy Desirable?

The worth of Proudhon's entire theory, as well as the foregoing suggestions for improvement, would be called into question if the value of autonomy could be convincingly denied. It is certainly not self-evident that the aim of reform should be autonomy. In fact, troublesome objections to its value can be raised.

One ground for belittling autonomy is that people do not want it. Few persons seek utmost freedom; most want only a basic minimum. A sufficient answer to this objection is: So what? The worth of ideals is not affected by conventional appraisals. It may be true that most people want nothing like utmost autonomy, for as the existentialists remind us, this is indeed a painful condition. But distaste for autonomy, however prevalent, cannot undermine its value.

Another argument against making autonomy the goal of reform points to its harmful psychological effects. "Where no body of common values and sentiments exists, a person feels isolated or lost," claims Sebastian de Grazia.[22] Erich Fromm agrees that an environment conducive to autonomy leaves man "isolated, powerless, . . . alienated from himself and others; . . . ready for submission to new kinds of bondage."[23] Sometimes explicitly,

[22] *The Political Community: A Study of Anomie*, Phoenix Book edition (Chicago, 1963), p. 4.
[23] *Escape from Freedom*, Avon paperback edition (New York, 1965), pp. 296-97.

more often by implication, such writers invite us not only to abandon self-direction as a value but even to infringe on whatever autonomy individuals now enjoy. J. S. Mill's venerable dictum about a man's own good never being a sufficient warrant for restraining him against his will is dismissed as inhumane, or even dangerous.

Even if autonomy were psychologically harmful, this would not logically require its rejection as an over-riding end. Anyone with a strong commitment to autonomy could treat the damage it caused as a necessary evil, to be tolerated for the sake of a greater good. Nor is an environment conducive to autonomy, though not compelling it, as psychologically harmful as some writers say. Persons who find self-directed action and choice debilitating are unlikely to engage in it, even when it is easy to do so.

The most serious objections to making autonomy a goal of reform are those which expose it as unreachable. One such objection denies that autonomy can be reached, on the ground that total release from external restraint is impossible. Removal of all outward impediments to action and choice would not emancipate them, quite the reverse. For men in a world devoid of political, social, and religious controls would be continually obstructed by one another's depredations.

Even if complete freedom from external restraint could be achieved, autonomy would still be out of reach, because release from external restraints would produce enslavement to internal ones. The phenomenon of internal restraint is quite genuine. The inner tyranny of habit, inhibition, and overwhelming desire can be as great a barrier to autonomy as the outward despotism of law, convention, and religion.[24] External restraint sometimes causes release from internal ones. Legal, social, and religious controls may help balance the psychological forces within a man, by strengthening some and weakening others, so that none overwhelm him. Hence full removal of external restraints would give rise to internal restraints that are equally inimical to autonomy.

Though these arguments show that complete autonomy is out of the question, they fail to disqualify it as a goal of reform. Though they show that autonomy is impossible to achieve completely, neither argument shows that it cannot be partially achieved. Hence anyone so disposed may make autonomy the aim of reform, provided he regards it not as a destination he will reach, but as a lodestar for guiding his search. What Proudhon said of the goal he aimed for is also true of autonomy. It is "an ideal to be pursued forever, but one that insuperable conflicts keep beyond reach."[25]

The elusiveness of autonomy may seem unfortunate. An unreachable ideal, after all, does not have much practical force. But this apparent defect is really a blessing in disguise. Confidence that ideals lie within easy grasp has been as great a source of human misery as despair of reaching them at all. Political wisdom begins with aware-

[24] Maurice Cranston, *Freedom: A New Analysis* (London, 1953), pp. 28-29. See also the interesting development of this theme, from a Freudian point of view, in Paul Roazen, *Freud: Political and Social Thought* (New York, 1968), pp. 289-99.

[25] Quoted in Daniel Halévy, *La vie de Proudhon* (Paris, 1948), pp. 392-93; cf. *Justice*, IV, 289.

ness that ideals are both necessary and unrealizable. It is complete when ideals, though recognized as unattainable, are applied to practice nonetheless. Whatever the defects of Proudhon's theory, it teaches this important truth.

# Index

# INDEX

Existentialists, 204

federalism, Proudhon's, 156-60; compared to Tocqueville's, 198

Ferraz, Martin, 5n.

freedom, Locke and Proudhon on meaning of, 19-22; respect and, 69-70, 73; deference and, 96-97; Proudhon and Rousseau on, 110-12; anarchy and, 118; bargaining and, 124; federalism and, 155-56; Tocqueville and Proudhon on, 197; autonomy and, 214-16

Freud, Sigmund, 55, 216n.

Friedrich, Karl J., 125n.

Fromm, Erich, 28n., 214

Gide, Charles, 171n.

Godwin, William, 104

government, as conflict manager, 41-44, 133; as civilizer, 50-51; as moralizer, 74; disrespectful, 94, 102-17; autocratic, 103-104; representative, 105-106; constitional, 106-107; direct democratic, 107-108; and price mechanism, 121; federal, 156-60; dictatorial, 172-73; and autonomy, 207

Grazia, Sebastian de, 214

Guizot, François, 97, 198

Gurvitch, Georges, 84n.

Guy-Grand, Georges, 11n., 84n., 184n.

Halévy, Daniel, 5n., 11, 150, 216n.

Halévy, Elie, 84

Haubtmann, Pierre, 24, 58n., 89n., 98n.

hedonism, egoistic, 30-31, 33; see egoism; Proudhon, his psychology

Hegel, G. W. F., 57-61

hierarchy, and social stability, 40, 42, 44-47, 133; as civilizer, 50; disrespectful, 94-101, 137-39

Hobbes, Thomas, 28, 29, 38, 118-20, 133, 161

Hoffmann, Stanley, 157n., 192n., 199n.

Hume, David, 31

inequality, see hierarchy

international relations, 145-46

Isambert, Gaston, 5n.

justice, distributive, 99-101, 136-39; commutative, 134-36; see respect

Kant, Immanuel, 90-93

Kateb, George, 191n.

Kendall, Wilmoore, 18n.

Lair, Maurice, 13n.

laissez-faire, 120-24, 171

Lakoff, Sanford, 101n.

La Rochefoucauld, François, 29

law, Rousseau on desirability of, 102, 112; Luther on undesirability of, 103; Proudhon on, 112-15; and laissez-faire, 122-23; as manager of conflict, 133, 151; and social pressure, 158, 210-11; as means to liberation, 211-14

liberalism, and Locke, 18; and distributive justice, 99-100; and federalism, 157-58

liberation, 20-21; and Proudhon's philosophy of history, 37, 49-54, 58-60; and bargaining, 124, 161-62; and respect, 200-203; and sociology, 205-206; and social diversity, 130-31, 210-11; and law, 211-14